JUNG &
FEMINISM

BEACON PRESS BOSTON

JUNG & FEMINISM

DEMARIS S. WEHR

LIBERATING ARCHETYPES

Beacon Press
25 Beacon Street
Boston, Massachusetts 02108

Beacon Press books
are published under the auspices of
the Unitarian Universalist Association of Congregations.

96 95 94 93 92 91 90 89   3 4 5 6 7 8

Text design by Linda Koegel

Library of Congress Cataloging-in-Publication Data
Wehr, Demaris S.
Jung and feminism.
Includes index.
1. Feminism.   2. Jung, C. G. (Carl Gustav),
1875–1961.   I. Title.
HQ1154.W43 1987   305.4'2   86-47864
ISBN 0-8070-6734-2
0-8070-6735-0 (pbk)

TO MY MOTHER, FRANCES STARK SNYDER

CONTENTS

PREFACE

In the summer of 1985, while teaching a course on depth psychology and religion at Claremont School of Theology, I had a dream in which I was endlessly currying a black and white spotted pony that stood on the floor beside my desk. To my amazement, it grew smaller and smaller under my ministrations, until it was quite small and all white. I put it on my desk with an unexplainable feeling of satisfaction that it could fit there.

Upon awakening, I felt dismay at the apparent diminution of the original beautiful pony so like the black and white Welsh pony I had owned as a teenager. With a little reflection, the meaning of the dream became clear. The black and white spotted pony represented my Ph.D. dissertation and the white miniature pony this book. The dissertation had been large, even unwieldy, while this book is small. In the dissertation were a number of "black spots," among which was my anger at the sexism I had found embedded in Jung's psychology. From the beginning of my acquaintance with it, Jung's psychology had meant a great deal to me. My experience of betrayal, disappointment, and anger was proportional—and real.

But my anger at Jung has dissipated in the recognition of his humanness. Perhaps we are most angry at those whom we hold in the highest regard when they fail to live up to their billing in our minds as gods and appear as the fallible human beings they always were. The transformation of dissertation into book represents a "purification process"—hence the miniature pony's whiteness. This book represents not only a diminution and a "purification," but also a working-through from opposition to dialogue.

Both the feminist and the Jungian perspectives are important to me and have been for a long time. Jungian analysis, and especially Jung's deep appreciation for the wisdom of dreams, has enriched my life immeasurably. Had it not been for feminism, I might never have completed my Ph.D. Mary Daly's book *Beyond God the Father* afforded me my first enlightened glimpse into my dilemma as a woman and a graduate student of religion and psychology. Daly articulated what I felt: an inherent alienation between my chosen field of study and my sex. Before reading Daly, I simply experienced my confusion as "my problem." As a result of the richness I have found in both psychology and feminism, my aim in this book is to build bridges in several senses: the most obvious is a bridge between feminism and Jung. This bridge, built on insights from feminist theology and psychology, can strengthen Jungian psychology's application to women. A parallel bridge links the disciplines of sociology and psychology. Feminist theologians and psychologists draw on the perspective of sociology, while Jung and Jungians fall squarely into the field of depth psychology—a psychology that emphasizes unconscious factors rather than social context in the development of personality.

The act of bringing together the perspectives of these two fields—fields not often in dialogue, given their presuppositions—has resulted in the play on words in the subtitle: "Liberating Archetypes." Critics of Jung's psychology, liberation thinkers among them, often dismiss archetypes as Platonic ideal forms—unchanging, static, and eternal. Liberation thought, of which feminism is one prominent example, starts with the context and experience of a particular group, not with universal forms or ideas. Liberation theory focuses on the particular and feminism focuses on the experience of women. Analytical psychology, in which the archetypes are the foundation of the psyche and of life, looks for, and finds, universals—and, according to its critics, excludes the particular, as well as the social context. Critics would also claim that universal categories function imperialistically; that they replicate the worldview and situation of the person or persons to whom they are "revealed," or who are reflecting upon them. Liberation thought and analytical psychology (and other depth psychologies) are thus not often found in dialogue. "Liberating archetypes," then, puts in the same subtitle two usually antithetical ideas—liberation and archetypes. I have chosen this subtitle to indicate that I will be bringing the light of liberation theory to bear on analytical psychology, thus "liberating" the archetypes from their static and eternal associations. Paradoxically, the subtitle suggests that archetypes are liberating—a possibility Jungians might embrace. For the play on words in the subtitle, and the fun we had thinking about it together, I am grateful to my brother, Dan Snyder.

The fields I draw upon and address are three: Jung (and Jungian psychology), feminism (especially feminist theory in religion and psychology), and religion (in particular, the religiousness of Jung's psychology). That Jung's psychology is a religion is the foundation on which my feminist critique rests. In chapter 1, I outline the tensions between Jung and feminism. In chapter 2, I explain certain feminist principles of scholarship and the use I make of these principles in this book. Also in chapter 2, I explain the perspective of the sociology of knowledge and show how it applies to religion. In chapters 3 and 4, I explore the relationship between Jung's life and his concepts. This relationship reveals the religious nature of Jung's terms, but it is in chapter 5 that I develop explicitly the line of reasoning establishing that Jung's psychology is a religion. In chapter 6, I bring feminist principles of analysis to bear on Jung's psychology and suggest revisions in a feminist mode.

Besides being a religion, Jung's psychology is in some ways a theology and an ontology. Since this is so, it can be addressed appropriately by feminist theologians, who, like Jung, explore the realm of images and symbols. Also like Jung, they cross the boundaries between the disciplines of religion and psychology. Throughout the book, I intend to maintain a tension between the value of Jung's concept of the psyche and the feminist critique. Divested of sexism, Jung's psychology is invaluable for an adequate understanding, not only of ourselves, but of the world. Jung's psychology is a worldview and offers far-ranging explanations, some of which are ignored at our peril.

My family and friends have provided inestimable support to me during this project. Many deserve special thanks. Besides my brother, Dan, I think first of Polly Young-Eisendrath, Peggy Sanday, and Maurice Friedman, all of whom provided that special combination of intellectual sharing and personal caring that means so much. Polly's love, boundless enthusiasm, and plenitude of ideas have become a part of my life and have nourished and challenged my thinking about Jung and feminism for some time. Peggy's tough questions, always with the aim of improving my work, and her efforts on behalf of my title are much appreciated. Maury Friedman was one of the men who originally "heard me to speech." He helped me think about possible titles for this book and sharpened some points I made about Martin Buber's critique of Jung in chapter 5. Last, but by no means least, I am grateful to Caroline Birdsall, senior editor at Beacon Press, who encouraged me, prodded me, and probed my meaning so that I got close to saying what I intended.

Each of the following knows why I am especially grateful to them: Carol Armstrong, Janet Briggs, Lelia Calder, Joann Conn, Peg Copeland, Kathryn Damiano, Mary Dewitt, Elizabeth Dodson Gray, Linda Egan, Gay Grissom, Patrick Henry, Deborah Huebsch, Coke Hewitt, Mary Hopkins, Maria Myers, Suzanne Noble, Dorothy Reichardt, Parker Palmer, Deborah Snyder, and Tim Snyder.

Finally, beyond thanks: David Hart and Kirsten Wehr.

1

JUNG AND FEMINISM: OPPOSITION OR DIALOGUE?

In his foreword to *Twice-Told Tales*, Bruno Bettelheim tells a story from his experience of teaching fairy tales to graduate students in psychology. Having had the students write down from memory a fairy tale that had been important to them in their childhood, Bettelheim asks them to reread the original tale and to compare it with their remembered version. Students are always startled at the contrast between their remembered tales and the actual tales. Bettelheim singles out one student for comment:

> Asked to recall her favorite childhood fairy tale, one student, a normal well-functioning person in her mid-twenties, wrote instead a diatribe against what she characterized as male chauvinism in "Hansel and Gretel." The story had obsessed her as a child and had continued to make her very angry whenever it came to her mind, which happened frequently.[1]

To make a long story short, this student remembered Hansel as completely dominating Gretel, to the point of believing that Hansel, not Gretel, pushed the witch into the oven. The student blamed the fairy tale for encouraging her passive behavior, which gave her brother a great deal of responsibility in and power over her life. She "in large part blamed this dependency on fairy tales such as this one, which she felt impressed girls

1

with the message that domination by older brothers—or males—is their inescapable lot."[2] The woman was dumbfounded to discover that in the original tale Gretel, not Hansel, pushes the witch into the oven. She refused to believe it. She searched and searched for the *truly* original tale, until she finally had to accept the fact that for psychological reasons unknown to her, she had constructed her own unique version of the tale.[3]

While Bettelheim may not intend to discredit feminism or this woman's feminist leanings (in fact, he does not mention feminism at all), in his account of her distortion of the fairy tale material, he implies that feminists (at least this one) project their psychological problems onto the surrounding context far more than is warranted.

Ann Ulanov, a Jungian analyst, likewise finds weaknesses in the position of many feminists, deploring the absence of introspection and self-criticism inherent in blaming others (i.e., patriarchy or men) for one's problems. She points out that such blaming robs women of their own authority, giving it once again to men. "Some feminists take up this position of woman as victim so vigorously that their conviction of woman's capacity for self-determination is belied."[4] "When we locate all injustice and unhappiness outside ourselves, we find a place to put all our negative feelings. Politicization, in contrast to politics, acts as an opiate for anger and anxiety. Rage becomes a weapon for social change. That the anger is excessive, overdetermined by unconscious causes, attacks the rights of others, and foments violence, is not important."[5] Perhaps Ulanov's most telling observation regards those feminists who wish to reduce sexual differences to socialization. In defense of the Jungian term "the feminine," Ulanov says:

> The origins of these symbols [of the feminine] cannot be traced solely to objects introjected or implanted from without. The argument against this position, that such a range of feminine symbols merely demonstrates a sexism that overarches the centuries appeals mainly because of its stunning simplemindedness. Reductionism on such a grand scale is an unconscious tribute to male power; it merely offers escape from the hard fact that the feminine element of being has been recognized for centuries. We may challenge the way it has been misused to abuse women, but we cannot avoid it or reject it.[6]

In a similar manner, other psychologists and psychoanalysts have "psychologized" the feminist movement.

Rosemary Ruether, a leading U.S. feminist theologian, takes an opposing view. She faults Jungian psychology for supporting men's "co-optation" of the feminist movement. Some men, she says, "become aware that the polarization of the sexes is a real issue. They leap quickly to the thought that men too have suffered from sexism; indeed they have suffered 'equally.' . . . They need to recover the 'feminine' side of themselves. Jungian psychology provides the intellectual base for this male 'feminism.'"[7] Ruether focuses her argument precisely on the "feminine" that Ulanov finds central and ineradicable in human life, and whose source Ulanov firmly believes cannot be traced solely to externals because it is universally present:

> In [male feminists'] identification of their own suppressed self with the "feminine," they think they have a handle on women's true "nature." They want women to cultivate this male definition of the "feminine" in order to nurture the "feminine side" of men. They purport to understand and sympathize with women and, no doubt, sincerely think they do. But they tend to become very hostile when women suggest that this definition of the "feminine" is really a male projection and not female humanity. The male ego is still the center of the universe, which "feminism" is now seduced into enhancing in a new way.[8]

Another prominent feminist theologian, Mary Daly, goes further than Ruether in condemning Jung:

> Particularly seductive is the illusion of equality projected through Jung's androcratic animus-anima balancing act, since women are trained to be grateful for "complementarity" and token inclusion. . . . Thus it is possible for women to promote Jung's garbled gospel without awareness of betraying their own sex and even in the belief that they are furthering the feminist cause.[9]

Thus the stage is set for unending conflict between feminists who discount Jungian psychology and Jungian psychologists who discount feminism. When people become adversaries it is easy indeed to attack each other's weakest sides, often—as in this case—with considerable accuracy. The battle lines are drawn and, it would appear, there is little ground for fruitful dialogue. In this kind of conflict, each side focuses only on the obvious weaknesses, without acknowledging or addressing the other's equally important strengths. In both cases, it seems, "buttons are pushed" and willingness to listen is suspended. But if one can listen to one's harshest critics, one can usually learn something. With regard to both Jungian psychology and feminism, the criticisms on both sides have some merit. It is their sweepingly condemning nature that lessens the possibility of mutual learning and dialogue.

For example, Ulanov's point is well taken that by blaming patriarchy for an unmitigated sexism, some women avoid examining the ways they accept patriarchy's definition of them. For their own unconscious reasons, they thus bypass awareness of their collusion with a definition of woman as victim. Ulanov's desire, if I read her correctly, is to free women from that kind of self-deceptive tyranny, to aid them in becoming mature and responsible adults able to choose not to be victims. But feminism cannot be dismissed as "stunningly simpleminded" in its analysis of the feminine. Ulanov has missed the intellectually complex and often brilliant nature of feminist discussions. For their part, many feminists condemn Jung for his androcentrism, and they are accordingly unable to admit the possible benefits of an in-depth understanding of the human psyche such as the one he offers. Ruether and Daly, for example, unsympathetic to Ulanov, claim that Jung's concept of the "feminine" does not adequately address women's reality, women's sense of who they are. Jung's "feminine," they maintain, becomes one more way of alienating women from their own selves. Both Ruether and Daly have done extensive research on the wounding of women (and men) by the pervasiveness of sexism, and as a result, they attempt to reverse androcentrism in their scholarship. (Androcentrism refers to an unconscious assumption of the male point of view as normative and results in naming the world out of the male perspective. This term, like other terms common to feminist thinkers, is explained in depth in chapter 2.) In very different ways, both Ruether and Daly speak with a woman's voice—a woman naming and claiming her own authority and defining her own categories. This reversal out of androcentrism into the centering in women's experience is extremely difficult for women to engage in for many reasons, not the least of which is habit. Perhaps the worst reason is the "punishment" women in patriarchal societies experience for going against the prevailing thought patterns. Daly and Ruether use a different perspective, hail from a different experience, and have a different primary agenda than Ulanov and Bettelheim. For Daly and Ruether, women's emergence out of the limitations of sexism is central. For Ulanov and Bettelheim, the reality of the unconscious, as it has been defined by Jung or Freud, is paramount.

Many women have found great benefit in Jung's psychology as it stands, needing no feminist revision. Some of these women, Ann Ulanov or Marie Louise von Franz, for example, have become Jungian analysts and authors. Scores of others attend Jung clubs, consult Jungian analysts, and study Jungian psychology. What is the appeal? In searching the writings of Jungian women for their personal experience of Jungian psychology, I found two who spoke directly to the issue: June Singer and Stephanie Halpern, responding to one of Naomi Goldenberg's early feminist criticisms. For both of them, the value of Jung's psychology is that it reinforces and illuminates their experience. Singer says: "My own personal experience has been that Eros, the quality of relationship has always come naturally to me, while Logos, the quality of intellectual discrimination and incisive confrontation in the world, has been something I have had to learn." She shows little appreciation, or even understanding, of Goldenberg's point that such tendencies are not "natural" but are a reflection of patriarchally inscribed roles. Later in the same article Singer corroborates Jung's animus model for women: "I have always looked upon my animus, my masculine soul, as being carried by those masculine-creative images in the world like Michelangelo, Leonardo da Vinci, Buckminster Fuller, William Blake, and others who, for me, have exemplified soul material in a very practical and concrete way." [10] Stephanie Halpern also defends Jung's psychology:

> I read with considerable dismay assertions by Naomi Goldenberg that Jungian psychology is "racist, sexist, and closed to new experience." For the past sixteen years of my life I have been involved with Jungian thinking as an analysand, in part as a teacher and in recent years as a psychotherapist. This has not been my living experience. . . . Jungian psychology taught me more of what I already knew as a young woman sixteen years

ago; that is, that I could not fit into the world view of my patriarchal fathers or worship their God in the ways set forth for me.[11]

Nonfeminist Jungian authors take for granted Jung's point of departure; Ann Ulanov in particular appears to find great profundity in Jung's vision of a psyche based on polarities, including sexual polarities (the "masculine" and the "feminine"). The primary appeal of Jung's psychology to women, it seems to me—based partly on my own experience—is that it is a "meaning-making" psychology. From within the Jungian framework, dreams, fairy tales, myths, and other forms of folklore contain wisdom and direction for our lives. Meaning is also found in dialogue with one's "inner figures," who present themselves in dreams. Jung's psychology can open up new worlds—not only those of dreams, fairy tales, and myth, but also of poetry, music, dance, arts, and crafts. For Jung, the unconscious was the source of creativity, and Jungian psychology often releases creativity hitherto unexpressed. Analytical psychology offers a balance to an overly rational, materialistic world and can shed light on the darkness of a soul lacking meaning. It can be the path to a person's spiritual awakening.

For nonfeminist Jungian women, Jung's validation of the "feminine" has great appeal. They find permission in his psychology to be "feminine," as well as to actualize their "masculine" side. In a world where women now compete with men on male terms, Jungian women (many of whom are successful in the "outer" world) feel vindicated in relying on what Jung would call their "feminine instinct." Jung defined the feminine largely in terms of receptivity—for Jung, receptivity is the sine qua non of religious experience, which links the feminine and religion as well. In classes where I have taught Jungian psychology to feminists, I have noticed that they frequently reject Jung's notion of the feminine and its corresponding receptivity. They argue that Jung is stereotyping women once again, depriving them of being agents in their own right. Jungian women feel just the opposite; they believe receptivity is a quality much needed in the world, and that it is a form of empowerment.

Both Jungian psychology and feminism function as ideologies and both are controversial. They galvanize one's deepest loyalties. It becomes difficult to think outside the parameters of either one of these worldviews once one is within them. Each contains a compelling explanation of the world as it is, and each meets the needs of its many adherents for understanding and order. In these ways and others, each one comes close to being a "religion." Indeed, as I shall explore in depth in a later chapter, the religiousness of Jung's psychology is an important part of its appeal and its strength.

In some measure this conflict reflects an ongoing tension between the disciplines of sociology and psychology, since many feminist theologians draw on the assumptions of sociologists. At the risk of oversimplification, one could say that sociology seeks an explanation of the world, of society, and of individual psychology in social (group) forces, while psychology's explanations focus primarily on causes within the individual psyche and extend them to society at large. Therefore, from the perspective of depth psychology, to understand society one must understand the psyche. For Jung, this means understanding the collective unconscious that embraces all of humanity. It is the "sea" on which the individual unconscious and conscious rest. It contains "qualities that are not individually acquired but are inherited, e.g., instincts as impulses to carry out actions from necessity, without conscious motivation." [12] This Jungian concept is actually a bridge between sociological and psychological explanations, since it takes in both the individual and the collective. But it is often understood as operating a priori and ontologically, rather than sociologically, and therefore as being in conflict with sociological views.

SYNTHESES

Attempts at synthesis have come, for the most part, from academicians, especially feminist theologians. However, there are some Jungian analysts who use feminist insights, such as Sylvia Brinton Perera and Linda Leonard; and there is at least one self-identified feminist Jungian analyst, Polly Young-Eisendrath. One of the most thorough attempts at integrating feminist thought and Jungian psychology is an anthology edited by Estella Lauter and Carol Schreier Rupprecht. In their introduction and conclusion, as well as in their essays and those of the other authors, Lauter and Rupprecht examine the significance of an archetypal unconscious in women's lives today, returning again and again to women's lived experience for corroboration. Lauter and Rupprecht recommend "unconsciousness raising," and a multidisciplinary approach to feminist theory-making.[13]

Naomi Goldenberg and Carol Christ are two feminist theologians who also have attempted to bridge the gap between the two points of view. Both of them have criticized Jungian psychology from a feminist perspective, yet each has retained elements from depth psychology that she feels are essential to an understanding of the human condition and to a renewal of life on this planet.[14] Christ makes the point that Jungian psychology addresses the situation of the male quite well, but that it offers an inadequate portrait of the female psyche.[15] I will expand on this point in chapter 6. Goldenberg recommends that feminists retain Jung's vision of the importance of myth, ritual, and symbol in human life. She finds Jung's method of working with dreams promising, and she focuses on the role of dreams, fantasies, and visions in a feminist mode.[16] Yet these women have not been widely accepted among Jungians, perhaps because they have identified themselves as feminists. Goldenberg says, "I am often termed *animus-ridden* when I speak to Jungian audiences about the logical flaws in the anima/animus theory. No matter how demurely I dress for a lecture, I am sure to be warned about departing too far from femininity as soon as I raise doubts about the universality of inferior Logos in women."[17] ("Animus-ridden" is a term we will cover in chapter 4. In short, it is a term that casts aspersions on a woman's femininity, claiming that she has not integrated her animus—her unconscious, masculine side—and is therefore "possessed" by it, "acting like a man.")

My position is closer to that of Goldenberg and Christ than it is to either an orthodox Jungian one or to the sort of feminism that condemns all male systems of thought as fatally flawed. I believe that both feminism and Jungian psychology contribute significantly to an understanding of the human situation. Jungian psychology is a meaning-giving psychology. It does not reduce the human condition to pathology. In fact, it has the happy tendency to see symptoms as symbolic of the psyche's effort to redress an imbalance, to right an unconsciously felt wrong. Jung's view of the contemporary world situation offers the most complete psychological/spiritual explanation of it I know. His advocacy of the withdrawing of projections (no longer seeing in others what are really our own characteristics) as a prerequisite for getting along—whether it be between nations or between individuals—seems to me to contain a wisdom crucial to world, and to individual, understanding.

FEMINIST PERSPECTIVES

So many perspectives hold sway within feminist theory that to use the term feminism as if it meant one thing is misleading. Feminists themselves debate over whether or not patriarchy (literally, "government by the fathers") is and always has been universal.[18] Whether patriarchy can be seen as universal, however, is not my concern here. Interestingly, male dominance in Western culture, if not the universality of patriarchy, is a topic on which Jungians and feminists agree. That agreement will be my starting point: patriarchy, understood as male dominance of public life and thought-systems, exists in Western culture and is reflected in all its institutions, including religion, psychology, and language. This does not mean that women have no power at all in patriarchy. Some women do, but it exists primarily in a distorted form and, more often than not, in the private sphere. The issue of the kind of power women exert will be examined in a later chapter, in an application of feminist insights to Jungian terms.

Another unresolved tension in feminist thought is whether men and women are fundamentally the same or different (beyond basic biological differences). Many Jungians, among them Ann Ulanov, seem to fear that feminists wish to obliterate all differences between men and women. The fear is unfounded. Nevertheless, the question of whether differences between the sexes are socially constructed or biological remains unsettled among feminists themselves. Feminists of the "social construc-tionist school" agree that there are differences acted out in the lives of males and females, but they say that these differences are socially constructed and not biologically determined. The so-cially constructed differences, they believe, have been socially useful. Adherents of this school believe that to identify certain personality traits as innately masculine or feminine, as some other feminists do, legitimates the universality of male dominance. Paradoxically, they fear that the "innate difference school" will be used to discredit men and the masculine way of being in the world, just as the old, patriarchal view of innate differences has been used to discredit women and the "feminine." Their deepest fear, however, is that the "innate difference school"— even if used by feminists to validate the "feminine"—will simply reify differences between the sexes and will ultimately be used in the way it always has been, to discredit women.

Most feminist theologians today discuss differences in male and female behavior and values. Like Carol Gilligan in psychology, feminist theologians often note that what has been denigrated in patriarchy as "feminine" behavior has, in fact, some strengths. Also like Gilligan, they may not discuss the origin of the differences. A feminist view like Gilligan's could be seen as close to Jung's, but there is an important distinction between the two: for Jungians the feminine is indeed biological, innate, even ontological. Among feminist theologians, Mary Daly comes the closest to an innate differences model, and Rosemary Ruether to a social constructionist one. But, although Daly's position comes close to the Jungian view in that she appears to embrace the idea of innate differences, she would not define female characteristics in the same way that Jung does the feminine. Indeed, she is vehemently opposed to Jung's definitions.[19]

This debate, too, about whether differences between the sexes are "natural" or "cultural" is one I do not wish to enter. The full evidence regarding the roles of nature and culture in creating feminine and masculine behavior will probably be largely anthropological and is not yet in.[20] I will, however, draw on the social constructionists' insights about the way in which Western, patriarchal culture has defined the feminine. The plagues of sexism, misogyny, and the subtle, yet pernicious effects of androcentrism in society and consequently in scholarship, including in the fields of religion and psychology, have been amply documented.[21] I will focus instead on a particular aspect of patriarchy's wounding of women's self-esteem: internalized oppression and how it can be fostered by Jungian psychology as it stands. "Internalized oppression" refers to the process by which women internalize patriarchal society's definition of themselves. This definition is oppressive, negative, and inferior in many ways, although it is also often compensatory and romantically "exalted." Women learn to oppress themselves inwardly with patriarchy's alienating assessment of them. In order to work well with women who have grown up in patriarchy, therapists, including Jungian analysts, need to be supremely conscious of the reality of sexism and the probability that a female client will be suffering from its internalization. The following criterion for analysts working with women will be our guide.

> Sexism and its psychological companion in women, internalized oppression, are still so widespread in our society that any psychological theory and practice which does not take those facts into account and oppose them unrelentingly is not a freeing therapy for women.[22]

Recognizing the reality of sexism and its effects in the lives of women means taking seriously the patriarchal context in which we live and its ongoing effect in the shaping of women's and men's personalities. This will mean bringing the archetypal images "down to earth," grounding them in their social context.

2

FEMINIST THEORY IN PSYCHOLOGY AND THEOLOGY

Certain principles of feminist theory appear to be in conflict with the outlook of Jungian psychology. It is my contention, however, that the theory and practice of Jungian psychology in the lives of contemporary women would be strengthened and enriched if it was informed by these feminist principles. As we will see, the feminist approach focuses on the force of the social context in determining social behavior. Ann Ulanov, by contrast, is typically Jungian in her reliance on a biological and ontological explanation for social behavior. If behaving in a "feminine" manner, for example, is biologically, genetically, and even ontologically determined, then certainly women who do not act that way are violating their own natures. This is what the Jungian view of the "feminine" and the "masculine" implies. Yet, as we shall see when we explore them in depth, these concepts contain a high measure of ambiguity. They are not gender-specific; each one represents a potential for development in each sex.

Feminist theologians and psychologists, drawing on the sociology of knowledge and anthropology, focus on the context that shapes behavior. They have examined this context and its influence on our speech, patterns of thought, and behavior, and on our fears of being "different" if we dare to risk stepping outside of the rules our society holds for decent social behavior. They have appropriately labeled late-twentieth-century American society "patriarchal," literally, as I have noted, rule by the fathers. There are numerous consequences, for women, of living in a patriarchal context. Although these consequences have been amply discussed by others, it is important here to touch on them again in order to set the terms of our conversation in this book.

Jungian psychology's view of the human being is nearly "contextless." Archetypal factors that transcend time and space (and thus transcend context) are seen as the main shaping forces in individual personality. Exactly how much strength the social context has in shaping behavior and personality is not settled in anybody's mind. However, a contextless, timeless, universal, and ahistorical psychological theory, which one reading of Jung's psychology suggests, is bound to be viewed with suspicion in our day. My position in this book, drawing on the sociology of knowledge, especially as it has been articulated by Peter Berger, is that human beings are shaped by an "ongoing conversation" between themselves and significant others in their society, and that to step out of that conversation is to risk anomie.[1] "Anomie" is a term Berger coined, starting with Durkheim's concept of *nomos,* to describe what it is like to be without an organizing principle that gives meaning, order, and stability to human societies and life. To be without a nomos is to experience the sheer terror of nonbeing. Berger's view, and that of other social psychologists and sociologists of knowledge, addresses the urgency of acceptance by one's group in a way that Jung's psychology does not.[2] In fact, the "ongoing conversation" telling us who we are exerts a by no means negligible influence on our behavior, since we all aim for acceptance and inclusion in our social group.

SEXISM AS WORLDVIEW

The themes of sexism, misogyny, and the oppression of women are well-known, although their reality and their seriousness have not been widely acknowledged and accepted in our society. That lack of recognition stems from several sources, but one of the deepest is that sexism constitutes a worldview; that is, it is a "lens" through which one views the world and its rightful order.

That a lens may distort is not evident until the world it orders can be compared with the view through another lens—or through no lens. Women rely on the standard Western lens on the world nearly as much as men, since women, like men, have been socialized into acceptable behavior in this society. Further-more, there are rewards for women in accepting the sexist world-view if they fit nicely into it. For example, being found attrac-tive and appealing to men gives many women a feeling of worth (which patriarchal standards have deprived them of in them-selves). Attractiveness becomes literal value on the marriage market if one is looking for a man to support one financially. Success in being "feminine" relieves women of the responsibil-ity for developing their capacities for intellectual endeavors or certain kinds of strength. Unfortunately, these "rewards" do not usually satisfy for a lifetime. Women, like men, need to develop strengths and capacities for living in the world, if not for eco-nomic reasons, an increasing pressure, then for reasons of self-esteem.[3]

Let us touch lightly on the distortions in worldview that sexism imposes. Sexism consists of limiting beliefs about the "natures" of women and men. Although it is damaging to men, it is particularly wounding to women because women are the ones who stand outside of the definition of the fully human that maleness in Western patriarchy has come to represent. Because this is so, because it is reinforced constantly by the various levels of the "ongoing conversation" in patriarchy—in religion, in psychology, in popular culture—women find many difficulties in claiming adult status, responsibility, and authority.[4] Because maleness is normative and represents the fully human, women who choose to be a fully human adult are in a double bind with regard to their "femininity." Their "femininity," while not fully adult, guarantees their acceptance in this society.

As a worldview, sexism has come to be isomorphic with the structures of our consciousness. Looking through the sexist lens means that the sexist structures of society seem to be the way things are naturally. Anything that appears to be in the natural order of things comes close to being perceived as divinely or-dained and maintained, as Simone de Beauvoir and others have cogently demonstrated.[5] If the sexist order of things is "natu-ral," then it appears not to have been constructed by anyone, and thus to be an outgrowth of our biological or genetic natures. Such a belief lends deep support to the social order, and the structures of consciousness come to reflect the social order in which male privilege is entrenched. Sexism thus supports the privilege of males, many of whom would hate to lose that privilege. Finally, sexism conceals a deep fear of the female. We will explore that fear and its possible origins in chapter 6.

In Western patriarchy, the sexist worldview has resulted in the oppression of women. The external oppression of women, the visible oppression, often takes the form of exclusion of women from the public realm, the realm that carries prestige and that it takes "realistic toughness" (a quality "feminine" women are not likely to have) to manage. Thus women are excluded from government and high-level decisionmaking, from the top echelons of church and academic institutions, and from political and economic structures. Their exclusion from these quarters further reinforces male dominance there, which feeds women's reluctance to enter these arenas. Certainly some women have entered all of these domains, but the numbers have been so few that they represent a kind of token inclusion.[6] Another well-known form of the oppression of women in our society is the simple fact of less pay for equal work, and the fact that housework, or other "feminine" labor is devalued. Public worth is measured according to a masculine standard.

Androcentrism is a particularly pernicious form of sexism because of its potential for annihilating women's sense of selfhood. Androcentrism is, in short, the habit of thinking about the world, ourselves, and all that is in the world from the male perspective. From this perspective, the male is the center of experience, and that experience is normative.[7] The male norm parades as universal, and by that norm women are defined as "other," not center, as "object," not subject. Androcentrism drowns or silences women's voices and perceptions by the continual pouring-out of male perceptions into the world. It conveys the message of women's inferiority to them on a subtler, deeper level than does simple negative treatment or belittlement. The use of male generic language perpetuates the habit of androcentrism. Once women are defined and treated as object and not subject, as not normative, and not fully adult, the definition itself alienates women from a sense of authenticity and subjecthood. Definitions and categories exert great suggestive power since they tell us what is in the nature of things. Unthinkingly and uncritically we accept them, at which point they begin to function as self-fulfilling prophecies. This is why liberationist groups have focused on the importance of experience. By relying on their own experience, and not on what someone from the ruling group tells them their experience is (or should be), "minorities" have come increasingly to trust themselves and, as a result, to be able to challenge prevailing social definitions.[8] These definitions depend upon sufficient agreement for their continued existence. Of course, what constitutes "experience" is tricky, since it is in large part formed by the social and linguistic matrix out of which one springs. Many excellent discussions exist of the problem inherent in defining what "women's experience" is, and the formative role patriarchy may play in determining it.[9]

Polly Young-Eisendrath says: "I have yet to encounter an adult woman who did not evaluate herself in some highly convincing way as uniquely deficient or inadequate."[10] Her statement, stark in its implications, will serve to launch our exploration into another aspect of the consequences of sexism as a worldview. With sexism as an unconscious, hidden, yet everpresent part of the ongoing conversation in this society about the natures of men and of women, women imbibe daily messages about their inferiority. They sense that they risk severe punishment by going against the prevailing ethos. The very worst punishment a society can inflict on its members is exclusion. In primitive societies, as is well known, if a deviant member is excluded from the group and especially if this member is subjected to rituals of exclusion with intent to kill, the member usually dies. I think this realization has to be an important part of the analysis of why women themselves "choose" to internalize a sense of their own inferiority rather than challenging society's mixed message about who they are, which would start by challenging their feelings of inadequacy, since those feelings legitimate their subordinate status in the social order. Women sense, at some deep level, that they are acting in a "taboo" manner if they do not engage in the same conversational terms as everyone else. Although in primitive societies the punishment for transgressing a taboo is death, in our "civilized" society we do not punish deviants in this overt way. We simply snub them, refuse to offer them hospitality or understanding, and cause them a "death of the soul" rather than physical death. This is one of the reasons women who have engaged in the challenge feminism poses to society's categories have found support from other like-minded women. Without a social group one dies, spiritually or physically.

INTERNALIZED OPPRESSION

Women's sense of themselves as in some way "uniquely deficient or inadequate," feminists believe, is the result of internalizing patriarchal society's definition of them. Whereas for Jungians, the source of personality is found largely in archetypal factors writ large in society, the position I will take is that society and the individual psyche are in dialectical relationship with one another. That means that, as Jungians hold, psychological forces (prerational images, mythic themes, fears, needs) do indeed shape society. At the same time, social structures already in existence at the time of each individual's coming into the world exert great influence in shaping the individual personality. My analysis, like feminist analyses generally, credits the social context with more shaping influence than Jungian psychology usually does. The serious wounding to women's self-esteem of which Young-Eisendrath is speaking, I have referred to as "internalized oppression." [11]

Internalized oppression feels a certain way inside a woman, it speaks with a certain voice, and it has a certain effect on her. Doris Lessing's description of the "self-hater" in *The Four-Gated City*, as exemplified in the lives and psyches of her heroine, Martha Quest, and Martha's friend, Lynda, is an excellent illustration of internalized oppression at work. [12] Lessing brilliantly juxtaposes Martha's self-conscious encounter with the self-hater and Lynda's lack of awareness of her own victimization by this inner figure. [13] The difference between consciously confronting inner voices and simply being at their mercy without knowing what they are and without being able to differentiate oneself from them is great. Being able to make this distinction is, in fact, one of the main goals of a Jungian analysis. The following quotation illustrates both the self-hater's voice and effect and the disengagement of consciousness that allows Martha to observe its effects on her:

> Martha was crying out—sobbing, grovelling; she was being wracked by emotion. Then one of the voices detached itself and came close to her inner ear: it was loud, or it was soft; it was jaunty, or it was intimately jeering, but its abiding quality was an antagonism, a dislike of Martha: and Martha was crying out against it—she needed to apologize, to beg for forgiveness, she needed to please and to buy absolution: she was grovelling on the carpet, weeping, while the voice uttered accusations of hatred.[14]

A little later in the book, Martha consciously enters into relationship with the self-hater: "As she entered the country of sound she encountered head-on and violently the self-hater . . . yes of course she had half expected it, was even hoping to; but oh how powerful an enemy he was, how dreadfully compelling, how hard to fight."[15]

If, as Young-Eisendrath's words imply, all adult women in patriarchy have to contend with the self-hater, and yet do not know of its existence as an "inner voice" and have not distanced themselves from it sufficiently to "dialogue" with it or exorcise it, we can begin to estimate the amount of damage done to women by internalized oppression. Lessing ascribes Lynda's insanity to the ubiquitous, but unrecognized, presence of the self-hater. Most women in patriarchy who are not insane experience the unrecognized self-hater as depression, low self-esteem, too much dependency on others for approval, and a great fear of overstepping the place patriarchy has prescribed for them. The self-hater, or internalized oppression, is a crippling factor in the psychology of patriarchal women. Mary Daly calls it a "psychic embed."[16]

Examples abound in current feminist psychological writings about this vicious voice and its effects in women's lives. Jean Baker Miller has developed guidelines for a psychology of women in terms of our society's male domination/female subordination pattern and its effects on our psyches and behavior. She points out that "subordinates themselves can come to find it difficult to believe in their own ability. The myth of their inability to fulfill wider or more valued roles is challenged only when a drastic event disrupts the usual arrangements."[17] She sees such a "drastic event" in the eruption of World War II, for example, when "incompetent" women suddenly "manned" the factories with great skill. The usual categories of competence in our society deny women such ability. Miller persists: "Tragic confusion arises because subordinates absorb a large part of the untruths created by the dominants; there are a great many blacks who feel inferior to whites, and women who still believe they are less important than men." [18]

Mary Daly's most recent works have focused on the activity of internalized oppression upon women's psyches, as well as on the forms of external oppression that foster it. The significance of Daly's work lies, like Lessing's, in her stunning analysis of the way in which this voice cripples women from within. For surely, despite the strength of patriarchal society, with its fear of women and of what Jungians call the "feminine," if women themselves had not internalized damaging messages about their "inferior," "weak," or otherwise inadequate natures, patriarchal standards could not persist. Therefore, it is on the inner level that this voice wreaks the most havoc, since it paralyzes women from within, causing them to collude in their own destruction, or at a lesser degree of intensity, to accept their own lack of development. Daly details level upon level upon level of the activity of the self-hater, showing its effects in the erosion of women's capacities, energies, and ultimately, their selves. She shows its numbing effect, and the ways women defend against their own inner knowing—a knowing that could bring them freedom from the clutches of this inner enemy. Speaking of the need to become "dis-possessed," Daly states: "Pathologically re-acting against her own endogenous powers of resistance to invasion, she sides with her invaders, her possessors. Her false self blends with the Possessor who sedates his beloved prey." [19] She posits what many feminists consider a "metaphysical" and "abstract" solution to the problem, but it is a solution that many "spiritual feminists" appreciate: "Therefore, we must consider the problem of this mind-pollutant and its cure, that is, Self-acceptance." [20]

The self-hater in women can operate as an inner voice or inner figure, as we have seen. It also shows up in women's dreams and is often projected onto actual men, or sometimes onto women, and it functions to reinforce the woman's already formed feeling of worthlessness. The person who conforms to her image confirms what the inner figure says. It is possible that if the woman changes her inner image, by dialoguing with it, befriending it, or in some cases exorcising it, the person's behavior will change. It is also possible that if she challenges the person's power over her, the inner figure will change. Jung's method of working with dreams and images gives women a handle on the problem and demonstrates effectively that "inner" and "outer" reality are intertwined and mutually reinforce—even invent—one another. As an example of the intertwining of "inner" and "outer" reality, consider how the early experience of incest creates a certain vision of men in the adult woman's psyche. Young children internalize messages about themselves and the nature of "reality" from their parents. They cannot do otherwise. If painful, secretive, "dirty" things happen to them in childhood, they assume they are responsible or bad. Because their parents seem omnipotent and omniscient, children assume they deserve the treatment they receive. If incest occurs at a very young age, girls tend to block the memory of it, or dissociate, as a means of defense. In the case of father-daughter incest, they know at some level, nonetheless, that father has violated them and that mother has allowed this to happen. One of the many effects adult women retain of this experience is the inner, accusing voice—a result of their subjection at such an early age to the confusing cruelty of their parents. The self-hatred that this voice pours forth on women operates as an effective block to healthy relationships with men, perhaps, too, with other women, as well as to self-actualization in other spheres.

Feminist interpretations do not leave women in a state of perpetual victimization, as some Jungians fear, by locating the cause of internalized oppression in the surrounding context. Nor are these feminist arguments utopian or naive in their explanation of this sort of evil, projecting it entirely onto men in just the reverse way that patriarchy has projected it onto women. Blaming patriarchy and naming its effects in women's lives are two different activities. Accurate observation of the factors producing psychological traits is a first step in defining an adequate therapy for them.

THE POWER OF SYMBOLS

Symbols and images operate preverbally and prerationally and find their way into the thought-systems by which we live, including the ones society sometimes holds as the most rational. Because of their preverbal, prerational, and often unrecognized character, they have great force. As feminist theologian Nelle Morton puts it: "Images have the power to shape styles of life, values, self-images, ecclesiastical and political structures in the same manner that subliminal images have created far too many black children inferior and white children superior long before they reached the age of conceptualization."[21] Internalized oppression in women has the power of this kind of image. It is far deeper than rationality and thought can reach, and therefore, rational thought, or even mere insight, is not powerful enough to silence it. In women, by the time oppression has been internalized, it has the character of fervent conviction.

Jungian psychology concerns itself largely with images and their power. Many feminist theologians, as well, have considered the power of images. A main difference between the two analyses lies in the feminists' awareness of the political dimension of symbols and the apolitical character of Jungian psychology—a lack of awareness that functions to reinforce the status quo. Carol Christ, in discussing the power of religious symbols, puts the issue succinctly: "Symbols have both psychological and political effects, because they create the inner conditions (deep-seated attitudes and feelings) that lead people to feel comfortable with or to accept social and political arrangements that correspond to the symbol system."[22] While Jung's psychology offers a powerful and important understanding of symbols and methods of working with them, it is also itself in some ways a symbol system with political and social ramifications and thus supports the gender-based social order from which it sprang.

Let us take stock of the conflict/dialogue between feminist theorists and Jung as it stands now. Although this will be clearer after we explore Jung's concepts, it is important to reflect briefly here on the explanatory elements of each that are in conflict. Jung's understanding of the source of symbols is the collective unconscious, which, he posits, is universal. Many feminists draw on Jung's theory of the collective unconscious for their understanding of the power of symbols, while rejecting Jung's claims of universality. The androcentric nature of the prevailing symbol systems—from which Jung derives his theory of the collective unconscious—prevents feminists from claiming full allegiance to or responsibility for them as they are presented to us. This is why many feminists have gone on a search for pre-patriarchal systems or for the goddess in prepatriarchal history, hoping to find historical remnants of a worldview that does reflect women's consciousness.

Images carry the sort of power they do, not only because of their preverbal, nonrational character, but also because of their frequent alliance with religion. Religious symbols convey to us many things, among which is a certain cosmic order as well as a social order.[23] Unlike secular social systems, religion grounds its rules for social behavior in the Divine. That is, it presents them as though they were given to humans by God. (The fact that in the traditional religions familiar to us it is God *himself,* not God herself or God itself, shows how intricately connected are divine and male authority.) The fact that God gives the rules makes it particularly difficult to go against them. Religion, with its reminders of the sacred, stands behind social customs and rules. The rules for living are presented as *revealed,* as is the symbol system, which makes them both above criticism. Tampering with either one is seen as "heathen," "heterodox," or "wicked." This is particularly true of authoritarian religions, where disobedience exacts a high price.

Religions are also meaning-giving, locating their practitioners not only within a sacred and symbolic cosmos, but also within a human community. As we recognized earlier, belonging to a community is fundamental to human existence. Religion has thus fulfilled extremely important human needs with its cosmic grounding of the social order and its provision of a meaning-giving community. The community reinforces each believer's commitment to the path they tread in common, strengthening at the same time reliance on the religious imagery of the particular tradition.

Among the rules for behavior that have been revealed by traditional religions are kinship structures, regulating commerce between the sexes, marriage arrangements, and matri- or patrilineality and -locality. In the religious traditions that have shaped Western social customs, certain attitudes regarding appropriate female and male behavior have emerged. Whether or not the secondary status of women is inherent and unchangeable in these traditions is one of several questions feminist theologians are wrestling with. Given the interweaving of social rules with religion—that is, with the Awesome, the Holy, the Numinous—we can see how deeply entrenched male and female roles become. As Peter Berger says, religion is an especially powerful tool of legitimation "because it relates the precarious reality constructions of empirical societies with ultimate reality."[24]

Feminist theologians have demonstrated the way masculine symbols of and language for the Divine legitimate male power and authority in society.[25] The continued use of masculine symbols comfortably masks our society's fear of women's authority and power. Vesting divine power in the masculine reinforces internalized oppression in women, giving it a sacred cast. As long as we live with masculine symbols for the Divine intact, we avoid the discomfiture that feminine symbols of the Divine tend to evoke. If we allow ourselves to change our religious language to feminine language, and to experience fully all the ambivalent feelings that change elicits, we can begin to comprehend the ambivalence we have toward the full power and authority of female being in general. We will begin to see the degree to which our feelings have been conditioned by the dearth of symbols of female authority in our society. If one is religious (or even if one isn't, consciously) one's world has been shaped by religious symbols. As Carol Christ has pointed out, in times of crisis even people who no longer believe in the religious tradition of their childhood tend to revert to the old symbols.

The importance of the foregoing remarks about the legitimating function of religion is twofold. First, if as I believe, Jung's psychology is a religion itself, we will find it fulfilling many of the functions of all religions, especially in giving meaning to the lives of its adherents and in ordaining certain kinds of behavior, locating them within a sacred and cosmic frame of reference. Its symbol system, with its emphasis on the "feminine" and the "masculine," can be seen as providing the ordering function needed in human life. Like many religions, its symbolic arrangements do not pose a threat to the status quo, although paradoxically, Jung's psychology does pose a threat to traditional Christianity. That is a whole different subject, which will be treated only lightly in this book. Second, I hope to illustrate how difficult is the task in which women are engaged, showing the depth at which symbols of the "feminine" and the "masculine" operate. To see beyond the false claims of androcentric religion and, at the same time, not to lose sight of the central importance of religion in human life, as well as to find spiritual paths that nourish women, is one of our most challenging tasks today. In fact, many people, and there are many women among them, find in Jung's psychology a revival of their lost spirituality. For that reason, as we explore Jung's symbol system in depth, we will be engaging it on two levels: on one level, as a device for unmasking the way symbols emerge from and operate in the psyche, and on a second, deeper level, as a symbol system itself, with all the dangers of legitimation of the social order such systems hold. We will concentrate in particular on making unconscious androcentrism conscious.

3

THREE
FORMATIVE
RELATIONSHIPS
AND
JUNG'S
MODELS
OF THE
PSYCHE

Jung's writings are prodigious and often shrouded in ambiguity. Thus it is not surprising that popular misconceptions about Jung's psychology abound. Nearly as numerous are clarifications of his work by his followers, who bring to the task much the same devoted attitude that religious believers bring to scriptural exegesis. None of the clarifications is entirely neutral; they are often apologetic for the Jungian position. The reading of Jung's ideas that I will offer in my next three chapters cannot claim total neutrality either, but I shall nevertheless attempt an even-handed presentation of Jungian psychology so that we can proceed with a common understanding. My goal in retracing what may be familiar territory is also to provide a social and familial context, a background, for the Jungian concepts. Such contextualization will give us ground for the feminist critique to come.

Contextualization of Jung's ideas is, among other things, a feminist act. It is also an act of iconoclasm. Jung has become an idol and feminists are idol breakers. When people have assumed the proportions of prophet, guru, enlightened one, or savior, as certainly Jung has in the imaginations of his followers, contextualization is iconoclastic because it locates the spiritual leader in time and space, squarely within a human history of relationships, hopes, dreams, and a social and religious background. If all of these factors are seen as having a powerful influence on the leader's vision, this allows for a more critical perspective on the ideas. Contextualization, both a demystifying and a demythicizing act, undermines the idolization of the leader. It can thus be a liberating act for the followers. The removal of projections of omniscience from the leader allows the followers to become more fully themselves. It is in this spirit that I pursue certain aspects of Jung's background here.

Jung himself provides a "context" for his psychology in his autobiography. Yet his emphasis is practically the opposite of a usual contextual approach. In Jung's telling of his life story, the archetypal images in the unconscious (mythic images and themes) provide the explanation for his life experiences, rather than the other way around. Jung was, at times, practically an Idealist in the Platonic tradition, although to understand him solely in those terms would be to do him gross injustice.[1] My focus is different from Jung's own: I shall look at the influence of certain relationships on the development of his theories. In the opening statement of his autobiography, Jung says:

> My life is a story of the self-realization of the unconscious. Everything in the unconscious seeks outward manifestation, and the personality too desires to evolve out of its unconscious conditions and to experience itself as a whole. . . . What we are to our inward vision, and what man appears to be *sub specie aeternitatis,* can only be expressed by way of myth.[2]

In spite of Jung's emphasis on the unconscious, which relegates social factors to the far background, in the history of Jung and Jungian thought, it seems the moment for seeing Jung in his social context has arrived. A second generation of Jungians have achieved more emotional distance from Jung than did their predecessors. These Jungians are able to stand back from, criticize, and expand in various directions on Jung's ideas without being thought "apostate."[3] From academicians rather than clinicians have come the most pertinent efforts at providing a backdrop for Jung's ideas, foremost among them James Heisig's *Imago Dei* and Peter Homans's *Jung in Context.* Heisig gives much needed attention to the chronological development of Jung's view of the image of God, while Homans examines in detail the social matrix that spawned Jung's psychology. Both

Heisig and Homans offer a welcome model for balanced scholarship on Jung. While they both contextualize, neither does so with the intent to attack—unlike previous attempts at linking crucial events of Jung's history with the tenets of analytical psychology, undertaken mainly by Jung's harsher critics with the desire to discredit him.[4]

The history of writing on Jung is indeed a fractious one. Jung has tended to elicit strongly positive or overwhelmingly negative reactions. Such polarized responses make one wonder what it is in Jung that invites them. The lovers of Jung—and their love is evident—almost worship him. His psychology meets "Jung-lovers" at the level of their own experience, that of their deepest, unshared fears and confusions about themselves. The Jungian worldview offers them a way to understand tangled relationships and to help heal chaos in the world. It speaks to a spiritual hunger. The "Jung-haters" puzzle me more. Perhaps their hatred has something to do with the very thing that gives the "Jung-lovers" hope. Anti-Jungians may sense an unwarranted idolization and too much self-importance in the "Jung-the-guru" phenomenon. They may resent Jung's spiritualization of instinctual life. In short, I wonder if they are irritated by the religious dimension of Jung's thought, particularly if they are committed to a worldview that they believe is more tough-minded and scientific. Clearly, the spiritual quality of Jung's doctrine is one of the major reasons, if not *the* major reason, for Freud's dismissal of Jung. Perhaps the polarized responses to Jung continue the ideological and personal tension that caused Jung and Freud to break off with each other.[5]

Homans claims that Jung's work embodies three major themes: reaction against Freudian psychoanalysis, reaction against modernity, and reaction against traditional Christianity.[6] My own focus will be on three relationships central to Jung's development—with his mother, his father, and Freud. As we examine details of Jung's relational life, we will find ourselves looking at conflict once again. This will be conflict as it was lived out in these three relationships, particularly with the two men, and as it found its way into Jung's models of the psyche. Looking at these relationships, it is not difficult to forge a link between them and a conflict/resolution dialectic that lies at the heart of Jung's psychological paradigm. This dialectic is both dualistic and nondualistic. In fact, there is a kind of wavering on Jung's part between dualism and a reaching-beyond dualism that is never resolved. The uniquely religious character of Jung's psychology is bound up with each of these relationships, but perhaps most of all in the dynamic with Freud, where transference and countertransference occurred but were left painfully unresolved.

Like Homans's and Heisig's efforts, my own look at context is not an attempt to discredit Jung. I do expect it will provide a challenge to a contextless and universal reading of the central Jungian concepts we will be wrestling with—anima, animus, and the feminine. I believe that by looking with care at three of Jung's most formative relationships, we will be able to discern the way Jung's later models of the psyche reflected his experience of the world. We will be looking especially for the feeling tone of the relationships and their effect on Jung and on his theories. For theories do reflect experience, whether or not they are acknowledged as doing so. "Universals" are always, at least in part, a statement of one's own worldview, which has been shaped by one's experiences, projected upon the world.[7]

JUNG'S TWO PERSONALITIES

Early in his life, Jung felt himself to be "split" between two sides of his personality, which, in his autobiography, he called personality number one and number two. Jung's mother was similarly divided between a "daytime" and a "nighttime personality." The "daytime personality" was reassuring, maternal, and filled with comfortable "animal warmth," while the "nighttime personality" seemed to have an uncanny prescience about things ghostly and spiritual. That Jung's mother's second personality had both frightened and fascinated him is obvious from his words: "By day she was a loving mother, but at night she seemed uncanny. Then she was like one of those seers who is at the same time a strange animal, like a priestess in a bear's cave. Archaic and ruthless; ruthless as truth and nature. At such moments she was the embodiment of what I have called the 'natural mind.'"[8]

Jung was fascinated with paranormal phenomena all of his life.[9] One of his earliest experiences with this realm—an experience of poltergeist—occurred in his mother's presence two years after his father's death. Besides the unsettling nature of the experience (an old walnut table noisily split down the middle with no apparent cause), the interaction between Jung's personality number two and his mother's number two presages a split between what Jung later calls the "rational" and "irrational" (also called "nonrational"). Here their two "irrational" sides were in communion. Since this sort of communication never took place between Jung and his father, we can surmise that a feeling-link was forged in Jung between the "irrational" and his mother: "'There certainly are curious accidents,' I thought. My mother nodded darkly. 'Yes, yes,' she said in her number two voice, 'that means something.'"[10]

Two weeks later another such incident took place. This time, in Jung's absence, the blade of an old bread knife had noisily snapped off in several pieces, again with no apparent cause. Jung relates: "My mother's number two looked at me meaningfully, but I could find nothing to say. I was completely at a loss and could offer no explanation of what had happened, and this was all the more annoying as I had to admit that I was profoundly impressed."[11]

Jung's first experience of his anima and the feminine—and this is the case with men generally—was with his mother. His wife, Emma, and his mistress and later collaborator, Toni Wolff, both became central figures further along in his development and in his understanding of the anima and the feminine. Jung's strong sense of privacy prevented him from disclosing much about his wife and from even mentioning Toni Wolff in his autobiography. As a result, we do not have detailed information about these two relationships, information that would help us understand Jung's own anima more clearly. What we do know from Jung's life is that he lived out a painful division, as well as an attempt to reach beyond it for healing, in these two intense relationships. He maintained an uneasy balance between the two women for years, and late in his life attempted to integrate Toni Wolff into his family. In Jungian language, Jung had a "split anima" (a split image of the feminine operating within his own psyche), which was expressed in his divided loyalty between the two women. One of the women, Emma, represented for him a "motherly container," and the other more of a "soul mate." Jung's split in images and experience—between the wife/mother and the sexual companion—represents a polarity not uncommon in the lives of Western men. It was one of many experiences of duality lived out in Jung's life that made its way into his theories. This is true not only for the theories written by Jung himself. We can speculate with some certainty, for example, that Toni Wolff's schema of the feminine archetypes, according to which the "Hetaira" (a man's sexual companion, lover, soul-sister) and the "Mother" are opposed to each other, had something to do with her experience with the Jungs.

Recently another of Jung's important anima relationships has come to light, this one between Jung and an early patient—a highly creative, fascinating, deeply troubled young woman by the name of Sabina Spielrein.[12] Knowledge of this third relationship, like the other two, would shed light on Jung's anima. Then we could see the elements of it that he projects into his theory of the anima and the feminine more clearly. Unfortunately, as is usual with patriarchal history, we know very little about the women's sides of the story. We can only conjecture. The intensity of these relationships tells us that Jung was involved all his life with the feminine and with real women, struggling to understand both and ultimately to come to terms with them.

The two sides of his personality, which Jung felt he inherited directly from his mother, had far-reaching ramifications. Like his mother's two sides, Jung's own split was between a "daylight side" and a "dark side." Number one personality was the light one, the side that lived in what Jung called the "outer world." Personality number one enjoyed itself, and was proud, ambitious, and fascinated with facts. Number two personality, the "dark side," like his mother's, "knew" things, was hungry for meaning, and embarrassed his more conventional side because of its lack of relatedness to the world. In spite of Jung's embarrassment about number two, it felt, for awhile, more authentic than number one did. Jung fed number two with Goethe's *Faust* and Nietzsche's *Zarathustra*. Number one was rooted in the practical considerations of the here and now. Jung described their interaction with agonizing clarity, saying at one point that his number two regarded his number one as a "thankless moral task."[13]

As Jung grew older, the conflict between his two sides intensified until it culminated in the agony of a career decision. A maternal uncle, a theologian, encouraged Jung to try theology, a notion Jung rejected summarily. His ambivalence and conflict about career lay elsewhere. (Notwithstanding, it is worth noting that theological issues were to preoccupy him all his life.) The tension between the very different predilections of personalities one and two grew unbearable until, finally, it was illumined and resolved by a dream.[14] As a result of this dream, Jung discerned that his task was to "shield the light" of personality number one by letting it take the lead. "In the role of Number one I had to go forward—into study, moneymaking, responsibilities, entanglements, confusions, errors, submissions, defeats."[15] Jung chose medicine as a career. Personality number two went underground for awhile. However, this was not the end of the matter, and a complete resolution of Jung's conflict would come only when he chose psychiatry:

> Here alone the two currents of my interest could flow together and in a united stream dig their own bed. Here was the empirical field common to biological and spiritual facts, which I had everywhere sought and nowhere found. Here at last was the place where the collision of nature and spirit became a reality.[16]

This resolution, which Jung felt was a true one because it involved both halves of the psyche, is an illustration of the kind of resolution to conflict that Jung credits as authentic. He came to feel that if people would be true to both sides of a conflict, a true resolution would emerge that would not be at the expense of either one side or the other. A truly new thing could come into being, through the working of what Jung later called the "transcendent function." This resolution of his two sides in the surprising choice of psychiatry as a profession (surprising because of the low esteem in which the scientific community held psychiatry) also predicts the unique way Jung would think about psychiatry and practice it. In psychiatry as Jung saw it, opposites such as nature (the natural world, "matter," and the humanity of the practitioner) and spirit (the psyche, images, thoughts) are brought together. So, too, are what Jung called "objectivity" and "subjectivity": the objectivity of empirical facts combined with the subjective element of the personhood of the psychiatrist. Jung later came to believe that the therapist must participate fully with the patient in the healing process: "With his specific prejudice, with the totality of his being, he stands behind the objectivity of his experiences and responds to the 'disease of the personality' with the whole of his own personality." [17] The implications of this stance require a great deal of self-knowledge and self-restraint in order to be effective. But with the requisite self-knowledge, it hints at what Martin Buber has immortalized in his term "the between." In Jungian psychology as Jung practiced it, and as it is practiced now, the healing relationship is constituted of this intersubjectivity informed by the "objective factor" of scientific knowledge.

Jung's divided experience of himself, especially as it took the form of one "other-worldly" personality and one "this-worldly" personality, foreshadows his later theory of the archetype and its relationship to the human being. It is as if personality number two were the archetypal one, "overseeing" the development and "interfering" with the life of the equally important, but more pedestrian, number one. In Jung's view, experiences of dividedness are not abnormal. He later posited a split between conscious and unconscious as part of every normal personality. [18] What is unique about Jung's approach to his split is the careful attention he paid to both sides of it. As the autobiography makes clear, he did not give in to the prevailing Zeitgeist of his time, or of ours, which would have meant ignoring, or trying to ignore, the "irrational" side of the conflict. Jung came to value what he called the "irrational" very highly. He saw it as compensatory to the rational, which he believed is dangerously overvalued in Western society. Emerging out of this small piece of Jung's experience is his model of a psyche that is potentially balanced and whole. It is a teleological view, optimistic and trusting in the power of nature itself to redress an imbalance. This is the model of the psyche for which Jung is best known.

Whereas Jung felt he inherited the two natures from his mother, from his father, a Swiss Protestant pastor, came a more dismal and more problematic heritage. Although Jung found him more reliable than his mother with her uncanny side, he gradually came to perceive his father as powerless and as intellectually and spiritually trapped. Because Jung's father was involved with religion, and because Jung himself was so interested in finding meaning, he turned to his father for religious explanations. Unfortunately for Jung, his father never went beyond the permissible boundaries of dogma, which Jung found sterile and frustrating. Three events in Jung's relationship with his father stand out for their special contribution to Jung's later view of religion.

The first is the well-known "cathedral fantasy," which happened when Jung was eleven years old, attending Gymnasium in Basel. The fantasy came upon Jung one radiant day at noon as he was leaving school, on his way to the cathedral square:

> The roof of the cathedral glittered, the sun sparkling from the new, brightly glazed tiles. I was overwhelmed by the beauty of the sight, and thought: "The world is beautiful and the church is beautiful, and God made all this and sits above it far away in the blue sky on a golden throne and . . ." Here came a great hole in my thoughts, and a choking sensation. I felt numbed, and knew only: "Don't go on thinking now! Something terrible is coming, something I do not want to think, something I dare not even approach. Why not? Because I would be committing the most frightful of sins. . . . All I need do is not go on thinking." That was easier said than done.[19]

Sleep was banished for two nights while Jung kept continual guard over his thoughts. In his mind, he was warding off evil, for he feared that if he allowed himself to articulate the lurking thought he would be eternally damned. For his parents' sake, he tried not to risk such terrible consequences. On the third night, his torment became unbearable. "*Why* should I think something I do not know? I do not want to, by God, that's sure. But *who* wants me to? . . . Where does this terrible will come from?" The eleven-year-old's precocious theological speculations led him back to Adam and Eve, whom, he reasoned, God had made and who had sinned nonetheless. Jung concluded: "Therefore it was God's intention that they should sin." Finally Jung decided that God was testing him in the same way he had tested Abraham by asking him to sacrifice his own son, Isaac.

> "Obviously God also desires me to show courage," I thought. "If that is so and I go through with it, then He will give me His grace and illumination." I gathered all my courage, as though I were about to leap forthwith into hell-fire, and let the thought come. I saw before me the cathedral, the blue sky. God sits on

His golden throne, high above the world—and from under the throne an enormous turd falls upon the sparkling new roof, shatters it, and breaks the walls of the cathedral asunder.

So that was it! I felt an enormous, an indescribable relief. Instead of the expected damnation, grace had come upon me, and with it an unutterable bliss such as I had never known.[20]

This experience nourished Jung's growing criticism of his father's sterile dogmatism. Note, too, its similarity to his career dilemma in his acceptance of both the "irrational" and the "rational" aspects of the conflict. Having followed his dilemma through to a surprising conclusion, and having thus experienced bliss, Jung felt that he had been obedient to God's will. The deepest questioning and trusting of his experience had resulted in abundant grace. Jung's father's obedience to forms and to the institutionalized church came to represent what Jung called "creeds," which he opposed to "religion." "Creeds" were sterile and dry; they were precepts in place of religion, which for Jung is always grounded in experience. Jung's negative impression of his father's religion, heralding this Jungian division, was well formed by eleven years of age. This dichotomy between institutionalized religion and experience became an integral part of Jung's later psychology of religion.[21]

Although it would be facile to reduce Jung's later psychology of religion to his cathedral fantasy and his disappointment with his father's unquestioning obedience to forms, we can see seeds of many of his later writings on religion sown in these events. They take fruit in Jung's understanding of God as having a dual nature, combining what we normally think of as "good" with what we think of as "evil." The cathedral fantasy occurred earlier than the events associated with his mother that are reflected in his view of the psyche as compensatory. By "compensatory," Jung meant that the conscious and the unconscious parts of the psyche together make up the whole. What is missing in one is contained in the other. This is why Jungians speak of the "wisdom of the unconscious," meaning that the standpoint of the unconscious is needed to make a wise decision, to assess a difficult situation, and to become who one is meant to be. In the cathedral fantasy, for instance, what was repressed was what was most needed to complement Jung's conscious thoughts. We can also see one of Jung's psychotherapeutic methods evolving, the method known as "active imagination." Using this technique, a person encourages, or allows, the unconscious to produce its fantasy or to make its statement in some fashion (such as in drawing, sand play, or waking dreams), as Jung did when he let the rest of the unwelcome fantasy come. In short, we are observing Jung's budding understanding of unconscious productions as meaningful.

The second fateful event had to do with Jung's instruction for catechism, personally undertaken by his father. Most of the instruction had bored Jung, but he became quite excited about the doctrine of the Trinity. Jung was profoundly disappointed and his faltering faith in his father suffered, in Jung's words, "a fatal blow," when his father said, "We now come to the Trinity, but we'll skip that, for I really understand nothing of it myself." [22] Later his confirmation ceremony proved to be a disaster, chiefly because Jung felt nothing. He concluded, true to his cathedral fantasy, that the living, breathing reality that is God is not to be found in the church: "'Why, that is not religion at all,' I thought. 'It is an absence of God; the church is a place I should not go to. It is not life which is there, but death.'" [23] This experience opened up an abyss between Jung and his father that seemed, to him, "infinite." Jung saw the whole event partly in terms of his father's personal tragedy: "All at once I understood the tragedy of his profession and his life." [24] The rest of the responsibility for his father's plight he ascribed to the failure of the institutional church.

Once Jung inadvertently caught his father at prayer: "He struggled desperately to keep his faith. I was shaken and outraged at once, because I saw how hopelessly he was entrapped by the Church and its theological thinking." [25] Later Jung came to believe that his father protected himself from thinking because "he was consumed by inward doubts." [26]

The alliance of his father with religion, which was one of Jung's consuming concerns, and his father's continual inability to satisfy Jung's spiritual curiosity, must have forged a frustrating link in Jung's mind. A very real element of the frustration, as is clear from Jung's statement above, was his father's entrapment in dogma. In Jung's opinion, the dogma prevented

Paul Jung from thinking, from questioning, and from fully living. Jung's need for a certain kind of father was not met, and he felt this as a deep loss.

JUNG AND FREUD

Imagine Jung's excitement when he first encountered Freud. The relationship between the two men began unofficially with Jung's purchase in 1900 of Freud's infamous new work, *The Interpretation of Dreams*. Three years later, Jung's excitement about Freud's work began to blossom. He found in Freud a corroboration of his own work on "complexes," psychological disturbances that he found he could measure with his word-association test. The test consisted of a series of words, of which some were neutral and others were emotionally charged (such as mother, father, dark). Jung discovered that some patients took a longer than usual time to associate to some of the words, and he deduced that in such cases a "complex" was operating. Reading Freud's work convinced Jung that the mechanism of repression was causing the delayed response. However, from the beginning of his acquaintance with Freud, Jung did not agree with him that the content of repression was always sexual.

In 1906 the two men began corresponding, and the relationship was confirmed by Jung's acknowledgment of Freud's importance to him. Jung had also completed editing his *Diagnostic Association Studies* that year. He sent a copy to Freud, who, it turned out, had already purchased his own copy. In the foreword to his 1906 essay "Psychology of Dementia-Praecox," Jung wrote: "If I, for instance, acknowledge the complex mechanisms of dreams and hysteria, this does not mean that I attribute to the infantile sexual trauma the exclusive importance that Freud apparently does."[27] The balance that Jung attempted to strike in his foreword, both acknowledging Freud's importance and at the same time maintaining his own point of view, characterized their entire relationship and in some ways contributed to its demise.

For professional and intellectual reasons alone, their meeting was portentous, but a highly charged personal dynamic was also present from the beginning. From Jung's side, Freud, one generation older, possessed precisely the capacities that Jung's father had lacked. Freud was intellectually rigorous and emotionally honest. Like Jung, he did not spare himself the hard questions. Jung had seen his father as nearly incapacitated before life's tasks, so the contrast between Freud and Paul Jung was striking. The emotional tension between the two men showed up immediately in the difference in their response times to each other's letters. Usually Freud responded right away, whereas Jung often took longer. For example, Freud wrote thanking Jung immediately upon receipt of Jung's gift to him. Jung responded to Freud six months later. Freud's second letter came again on the heels of Jung's, but Jung took sixteen days to respond. This pattern became typical, and was a subject of speculation for them both. Freud began apologizing for responding so soon, but said he did not wish to force an artificial delay. Jung, for his part, apologized for delaying and began explaining it by an "unresolved father-complex" toward Freud. We see from the very beginning of their association the two elements that would, in the end, cause them to part company in a bitter and tragic way. At a theoretical level, the two were in honest disagreement over Freud's theory of sexual aetiology of neuroses. At another level, they were involved in an entangled, intense father-son dynamic fraught with ambivalence, consisting of a yearning for closeness and understanding, coupled with the need to maintain distance. In the *Letters* Freud seems to maintain distance by posing as an authority. Jung finally "acts out" a rebellious challenge to Freud's authority. In the beginning, however, the libidinal glue provided by the father-son transference gave the relationship an exhilarating quality. This bond enabled the two men to live with their theoretical disagreements for several years. At one point Freud even formally adopted Jung as an "eldest son" and appointed him as his "successor and the crown prince" in the domain of psychoanalysis.[28]

In the autumn of 1909, Clark University in Massachusetts invited both Freud and Jung to speak. Before embarking on the boat bound for the United States, Jung and Freud met Ferenczi, who was also invited to the Clark conference, in Bremen. While dining together on the eve of their departure, Jung mentioned to Freud and Ferenczi his interest in peat bog corpses, which he had heard had been excavated in northern Germany. A fascinating subject for Jung, it turned out to be extremely upsetting for

Freud, who felt that Jung's interest in this subject, and his mentioning it during dinner, masked Jung's death-wish toward him. Freud's conviction of Jung's desire for his death actually caused him to faint; at least, this is Jung's interpretation of the incident. Another fateful blow to the relationship occurred during the boat trip. Jung and Freud had been sharing their dreams and helping each other to analyze them. At one point, Jung asked Freud for more personal information in order to interpret Freud's dream more accurately. Freud responded with "a look of the utmost suspicion. Then he said, 'But I cannot risk my authority!'" Jung continues: "At that moment, he lost it altogether." [29]

In *Memories, Dreams, Reflections,* Jung cites this event as a crucial turning point. If Freud would not engage in mutuality, Jung did not want the relationship. A father-son aura of authority and resentment was palpably present. The father, in this case, remained authoritarian. A kind of antiauthoritarianism (as seen in Jung's rejection of institutionalized religion), a great respect for individuals' ability to know for themselves what is right, has come to be a hallmark of Jung's psychology.

The next stage in what was by now a fated denouement came in Jung's letter to Freud of February 11, 1910. It seems the Oedipal myth was already being enacted, as Freud had been predicting. This letter introduced the third element in their relationship that would contribute to its demise, the subject of religion. Religion, for both Freud and Jung, was paramount— in opposing ways. It was the central fact of life for Jung, whereas it was the central illusion to be sublimated for Freud. In a well-known letter, Jung stressed that only religion can replace religion, and that perhaps psychoanalysis could fill the gap that the death of religion was creating:

> Religion can only be replaced by religion. Is there perchance a new savior in the I.F.? [the international fraternity of psychoanalysis] What sort of new myth does it hand out for us to live by? . . . 2000 years of Christianity can only be replaced by something equivalent. . . . I think we must give it time to infiltrate into people from many centres, to revivify among intellectuals a feeling for symbol and myth, ever so gently to transform Christ back into the soothsaying god of the vine, which he was, and in this way absorb those ecstatic instinctual

forces of Christianity for the *one* purpose of making the cult and the sacred myth what they once were—a drunken feast of joy where man regained the ethos and holiness of an animal.[30]

Freud's response to this letter was notably cool:

> Yes, in you the tempest rages; it comes to me as distant thunder . . . But you musn't regard me as the founder of a religion. . . . I am not thinking of a substitute for religion; this need must be sublimated.[31]

In 1912 came another of Freud's fainting episodes, again occasioned by what he felt was Jung's death-wish toward him. Jung reports:

> As I was carrying him, he half came to, and I shall never forget the look he cast at me. In his weakness he looked at me as if I were his father. Whatever other causes may have contributed to this faint—the atmosphere was very tense—the fantasy of father-murder was common to both cases.[32]

I have dwelt at length on three aspects of the Freud-Jung relationship—theoretical disagreement over the role of sexuality in neurosis, irreconcilable differences regarding religion, and especially the father-son dynamic—in order to set out the three unresolved elements that played such an important part in forming and solidifying Jung's later views, particularly his religious ones. That the father-son dimension was connected at some level to Jung's disappointment with his own father's inability to question religion is indicated by Jung's desire that Freud should consider psychoanalysis a new religion, "revivifying a feeling . . . for symbol and myth." It seemed he wanted his "new father" to fill the gap left by his biological father. Jung's original father was entrapped by dogma. His "other father," Freud, had a dogma of his own. It was his understanding of science, and it excluded the "irrational," which for Freud included religion. The well-known concluding words of Freud's *Future of an Illusion* are, "No, our science is no illusion. But an illusion it would be to suppose that what science cannot give us we can get elsewhere."[33] Jung's second father tragically failed him in exactly the same area as his real father had, leaving him to do what neither of his fathers could—to plunge directly and experientially into the unconscious (which, for Jung, was the source of religious experience) without imposing any assumptions about what this would yield and without warding off experience with dogma.

In January of 1913, Freud proposed to Jung that they break off relations—a proposal to which Jung acquiesced. The hurt and betrayal Jung felt are evident in the *Letters*. Freud, on the other hand, maintained a disdainful aloofness. In October of 1913, Jung heard that Freud had doubted his "bona fides," his integrity, his good faith. Jung does not specify the context for this wounding event, this final blow, but as a result he quit his position as editor of the *Jahrbuch*—a position with which Freud had entrusted him. His resignation marked the end of his relationship with Freud and with psychoanalysis. In February 1915, Freud published *The History of the Psychoanalytic Movement,* in which he concluded that Jung, like Adler, had founded a new religio-ethical system that bore no resemblance to psychoanalysis. Freud, harsher in his treatment of Jung than of Adler, claims that Adler's movement is more significant because, "while radically false, it is marked by consistence and coherence. . . . Jung's modification, on the other hand, disconnects the phenomena from their relationship with impulse-life; and further, as its critics (Abraham, Ferenczi, Jones) have pointed out, it is so unintelligible, obscure, and confused that it is difficult to take up any standpoint in regard to it."[34]

"After the parting of the ways with Freud, a period of inner uncertainty began for me. It would be no exaggeration to call it a state of disorientation. I felt totally suspended in mid-air, for I had not yet found my own footing." With these words, Jung begins the chapter of his autobiography entitled "Confrontation with the Unconscious."[35] Jung felt Freud's rejection so keenly that he withdrew from the world, maintaining contact only with his patients and family, to allow himself full involvement with his unconscious. This period lasted for five or six years and was one of intense engagement with "inner figures" he discovered and later named. Homans understands this break to have stirred up all the old conflicts, including the religious ones, with ensuing experiences that Homans calls "personal-mystical-narcissistic." During this time, Jung worked with himself experimentally as both analyst and patient—in somewhat the same manner Freud had done after the death of his father—discovering multiple ways to encourage dialogue with the unconscious, and learning more and more about himself. Jung's dialogues with his inner figures, of which the best known are "Philomen" (Wise Old Man) and "Salome" (a young girl, an anima figure), can only properly be termed "religious" in Jung's own definition of the term: "careful observation of the numinosum." Homans believes that the general schema of analytical psychology emerged out of this period, and that it bears the imprint of the personally religious mode of experiencing that Jung underwent at the time.[36] While it is true that the general schema emerged out of this period, the events in Jung's life had been leading up to the unique formulation of his ideas for at least ten years prior to the break, and with regard to religion, since his childhood.

THE BALANCE AND CONFLICT MODELS OF THE PSYCHE

The notion of two psychological models holding sway within Jung's thought is not one I have found elsewhere, although the evidence argues for such a view. The model of balance, in which the psyche is seen as a homeostatic system capable of readjusting itself when out of balance, is the one for which Jung is best known. The various dualities we have noted, from conscious/ unconscious, rational/irrational to spirit/matter, are all accounted for in the Jungian model of the psyche. As we have seen, true to Jung's own experience, resolution of conflict occurs when one is true to both sides of the conflict, allowing the resolution to emerge from the unconscious. The inclusive nature of the Jungian view of the psyche, coupled with the Jungian habit of presenting the theories in mandala drawings, has contributed to the balance model. It is also often seen as holistic.

Another model of the psyche emerged out of Jung's confrontation with the unconscious—a model that was influenced by Jung's relationships of conflict. This I would call a "conflict model." Conflict/resolution and dualism/nondualism live side by side in the two models of the psyche, in unresolved tension with one another.[37] Let us look at some of the evidence for this interpretation. Jung cites many other oppositions besides the ones we have noted: for example, a division between "inner" and "outer" experience, and the fact that every archetypal image consists of two poles—a "negative" and a "positive." Tension between the oppositions in the psyche is central to its functioning. As Jung said: "Submission to the fundamental contrariety of human nature amounts to an acceptance of the fact that the psyche is at cross purposes with itself."[38] The tension between the opposites takes many forms. One is the opposition the shadow presents to the conscious personality. Without this opposition, Jung argued, "the necessary tension would be lacking."[39] Jung goes on to discuss the need for synthesis that the opposition implies, and the fact that the psyche finally produces symbols that unify.

We can also look at Jung's model as a dialectic of conflict/ resolution, rather than as two models. It is important to stress the conflict side of the model, however, since its balance-resolution-harmony side is better known and contributes to a misreading of Jung. Jung believed that the cessation of tension in the psyche would end in death. Tension is life-energy itself: "For theoretical reasons as well there must be some such tension of opposites in the child, otherwise no energy would be possible, for, as Heraclitus has said, war is the father of all things."[40] Earlier in the same text, Jung writes: "The most intense conflicts, if overcome, leave behind a sense of security and calm which is not easily disturbed, or else a brokenness that can hardly be healed. Conversely, it is just these intense conflicts and their conflagration which are needed in order to produce valuable and lasting results."[41] This quotation leads one to accept the balance model as the accurate interpretation. Yet, in his correspondence, Jung emphasizes conflict: "Ultimately, we all get stuck somewhere, for we are all mortal and remain but a part of what we are as a whole. The wholeness we can reach is very relative."[42]

In some of his writings, Jung speaks of "reconciliation of opposites," even of bliss. Such language suggests that a state of harmony is achievable. In a letter to a critic who appeared to read his psychology as a search for such a blissful state, Jung had this to say:

Nobody has ever been entirely liberated from the opposites, because no living being could possibly attain to such a state, as

44

nobody escapes pain and pleasure as long as he functions physio-
logically. He may have occasional ecstatic experiences when he
gets the intuition of a complete liberation, i.e., in reaching the
state of *sat-chit-ananda*. But the word *ananda* shows that he
experiences pleasure, and you cannot even be conscious of something if you don't discriminate between opposites, and thus
participate in them.[43]

In Jung's model, both conflict and wholeness are necessary
experiences. The symbolic union of opposites is the reverse
image of conflict, given the inherent opposites in the psyche.
Wholeness and brokenness, unity and division, are both essential to Jung's view. Mandalas and the potential for wholeness
they represent should not be taken as the full model of the
psyche—they are but half. Wholeness is merely an archetypal
image in the collective unconscious, and like all archetypal
images, it has its opposite. On this subject, Jung says: "Multiplicity and inner division are opposed by an integrative unity
whose power is as great as that of the instincts. Together they
form a pair of opposites necessary for self-regulation."[44]

Jung's typology, which he developed between 1913 and
1917, the years of his "confrontation with the unconscious," can
be seen as an illustration of the conflict/resolution dialectic.
Jung's express purpose in developing the typology was to explain
seemingly irreconcilable character differences, which result in
an inability to understand or even tolerate points of view different from one's own. The need for the typology arose directly out
of Jung's painful break with Freud. He also explained the break
between Freud and Adler in terms of his typology, as well as the
usefulness of each of their three psychologies. Adler's psychology, Jung felt, was introverted and thinking while Freud's psychoanalysis was extraverted and sensation-oriented. For Jung
himself was reserved "the difficult task of creating a psychology
which will be equally fair to both types."[45]

Briefly explained, Jung's psychology of types assumes that
individuals have at their disposal four possible modes of apprehending the world. They are thinking/feeling and intuition/
sensation. Each pair of functions is mutually exclusive, since,
according to Jung's model, one cannot both think and feel at the
same time, nor can one intuit and sense at the same time.
Thinking and feeling are called "rational" functions; intuition

and sensation are "irrational" functions. Feeling, in Jung's typology, is a valuing function. It is not the expression of emotion; it means placing a high value on certain things or qualities. Thinking is the process of understanding through logical analysis. Intuition is the ability to sense the whole, whereas sensation is primarily concerned with details. Jung posits that each of us is born with one of these functions "superior"—that is, we operate with it naturally and easily. Two more functions are "accessible"; we can call on them and use them relatively easily. The fourth and final function Jung calls "inferior." It is not well developed, and when we use it, it tends to be overdone, inelegant. Since the inferior function is not under our conscious control in the way the other three are, it can "sneak into" our behavior unbeknownst to us in an "unadapted" way. Although Jung does not specifically link the typology to a developmental theory, he does say that "the problem of opposites, as an inherent principle of human nature, forms a further stage in our process of realization. As a rule it is one of the problems of maturity."[46] By coming to terms with the opposites, he includes making conscious the inferior function, which was unconscious before.

Besides the four functions, Jung posited two attitudes. These are well known, and have entered our common language with a slightly different meaning (and spelling) than Jung's: extraversion and introversion. For Jung, extraversion meant taking one's orientation from the object (another person, for example), while introversion meant taking one's bearings from within oneself. A complete description of these types and their interaction with each other can be found in Jung's *Psychological Types,* vol. 6 of the *Collected Works.* I have explained them very briefly here for two reasons. The first is because the typology is central to Jung's psychology and will be included in our feminist assessment at least obliquely. The typology illustrates part of the theoretical underpinning for Jung's later statements about the "animus-possessed woman," of whom we will have much to say later. If feeling is the primary function of most women—which it is in the Jungian view—then thinking will be most women's inferior function. Therefore, when a woman thinks, it is likely to be in an "unadapted," unpracticed way. The problem with this kind of Jungian explanation, which we shall find again and again when we get to the feminist critique, is that it gives a "natural" explanation for a behavior that has been strongly conditioned by patriarchal standards. Indeed, men have only allowed women to attend universities in the last century. Before that, and even in the beginning of women's attendance at universities, men believed (and women accepted the belief) that higher education would be harmful to their nervous systems or reproductive capacities. With such an impoverished social and educational heritage, it is no wonder women feel less than confident when they think and sometimes present their thinking defensively or apologetically. Furthermore, women sense the prevailing social atmosphere, which still does not value their minds, and this influences the quality of their thought.

The second reason I have included this discussion of the typology is because it illustrates the conflict/resolution model of the psyche. Jung's typological model of the psyche assumes an imbalance in each individual as the starting point, and it posits that certain modes of apprehending the world are impossible to engage in simultaneously. Each of us must work at making the unconscious function conscious in order to round out our inherently imbalanced situation.

The most important form of conflict for our purposes, and probably the most fundamental form of it for Jung, is the opposition of the sexes. In a discussion of alchemy, Jung reveals his view of the relationship between male and female. He viewed alchemy as a projection of unconscious psychic processes onto the act of transforming base metals into gold. He likened analytical psychology's core process—individuation—to alchemy for its similar transformative action.

> After the hostility of the elements has been overcome, there still remains the last and most formidable opposition, which the alchemist expressed very aptly as the relationship between male and female. We are inclined to think of this primarily as the power of love, of passion, which drives the two opposite poles together, forgetting that such a vehement attraction is needed only when an equally strong resistance keeps them apart. . . . Primal guilt lies between them, an *interrupted state of enmity,* and this appears unreasonable only to our rational mind but not to our psychic nature.[47]

The ramifications of this opposition Jung finds in multiple guises, ranging from matter/spirit (matter = feminine principle; spirit = masculine principle) to Sol/Luna (Sol = the Sun, masculine consciousness; Luna = the Moon, feminine consciousness), to Rex and Regina in alchemy (the King and Queen), to the conscious male ego opposed by the unconscious anima (the image of the feminine in the male psyche) and the conscious female ego opposed by the unconscious animus (the image of the masculine in the female psyche).

One of the most significant ways in which Jung posed the opposition, which he felt was central to human life, was as a tension between good and evil: "The view that good and evil are spiritual forces outside us, and that man is caught in the conflict between them, is more bearable by far than the insight that the opposites are the ineradicable and indispensable preconditions of all psychic life, so much so that life itself is guilt."[48]

Having briefly shown the role of conflict in Jung's relationships and pointed to a connection between his experience and the role of conflict, as well as its resolution, in his model, I shall now move more deeply into the concepts themselves.

4

INDIVIDUATION AND OUR "INNER CAST OF CHARACTERS"

Amplification is the preferred Jungian method of explaining the core concepts of analytical psychology. "Amplification" refers to the process whereby Jungians "circumambulate" a theme, thereby providing ever more possibilities of approaching it. Jung and Jungians love suggestive, metaphorical language, and some even claim that to use any other kind of language is to succumb to the ego's need for precision and clarity, thus losing the essence of the concepts. Here, in attempting to explain Jung's central concepts and using the same "linear" method that some Jungians have also used, I will give in to the ego's need for clarity so that we can continue our discussion with a common understanding.

Individuation is the core process in analytical psychology. It is the goal of life and the way one becomes truly oneself—the person one was always intended to be. Individuation is thus both process and goal. As the term implies, it has something to do with becoming separate and individual. This separateness means especially becoming distinct from (attaining a separateness from) inner compulsions and voices that operate on one unconsciously. The self-hater we discussed in chapter 2 is a good example of a crippling inner voice. Jung's individuation entails not only distance from, and perspective on, inner voices (known in Jungian circles as "complexes" and "archetypal images"), but also separateness from one's fellow humans, in one way especially. Jung was particularly critical of what he called "mob psychology," seeing in it enormous dangers for humanity in general. Becoming individuated includes the ability to remain separate from the psychology of the mob, since one thereby comes to know one's own unconscious "cast of characters" well enough to avoid identification with them and the ensuing enactment ("acting out") of their voices in a destructive mode. Jung conceives his core process as the achievement of distance from compulsions, or "inner voices," at the same time that he advocates "claiming" and acknowledging previously unknown parts of ourselves. He thus implies a double movement during individuation—both a claiming of the unconscious as oneself and a becoming distinct and separate from it, so that one is not at its mercy. While these movements may seem contradictory, they are not. Both involve becoming aware of the unconscious figures, "dialoguing" with them (a method I will describe), which simultaneously acknowledges their presence (i.e., "claims" them as part of oneself) and gives distance so that one is not identified with them. Images appearing in dreams and fantasies frequently serve as a vehicle for increasing self-awareness. In describing individuation, therefore, Jung often focuses on images. He does not, however, offer a critique of the sexism embodied in the images themselves. That task will be ours.[1]

For the following discussion, we need definitions of Jungian terms. In the definitions that follow, our entire conversation will be about individuation, for all of Jung's concepts relate to that core process.

A central Jungian term is the "collective unconscious," a name Jung gave to a common "psychic" base, which he believed unites all humans. He claimed that the foundation for this theory was empirical, since it arose from his observations of the psychological processes of mental patients. Jung had a nearly uncanny ability to understand the symbolism of mental patients' confused communications, an ability he later explained on the basis of their common participation in the collective unconscious: "Even the most absurd things are nothing other than symbols for thoughts which are not only understandable in human terms but dwell in every human breast. In insanity we do not discover anything new and unknown; we are looking at the foundations of our own being, the matrix of those vital problems on which we are all engaged."[2]

Jung distinguished between a "personal unconscious" and the "collective unconscious." The former, he says, consists of "everything of which I know, but of which I am not at the moment thinking; everything of which I was once conscious but have now forgotten; everything perceived by my senses, but not noted by my conscious mind."[3] The collective unconscious, on the other hand, consists of qualities

> that are not individually acquired but are inherited, e.g., instincts as impulses to carry out actions from necessity, without conscious motivation. In this "deeper" stratum we also find the . . . archetypes. . . . The instincts and archetypes together form the "collective unconscious." I call it "collective" because, unlike the personal unconscious, it is not made up of individual and more or less unique contents but of those which are universal and of regular occurrence.[4]

For Jung, the collective unconscious is the universal, collective matrix out of which we all live. It manifests itself in instinctual actions and their accompanying emotions, as well as in recurrent themes, images, and motifs. These Jung called "archetypal," another well-known, often misunderstood, Jungian term.

In 1946, late in his life, Jung made a distinction between the archetype and the archetypal image. Before this his attempts at talking about universal themes and images, and his calling them "archetypes," had led to the confusion of the two terms. It is not surprising that readers of Jung continually confused archetype with image, since Jung did so himself. Ambiguity had reigned in Jung's treatment of the archetypal images, especially with regard to their universality, until the 1946 clarification. At that point Jung claimed universality only for the archetype, not the image, and made it clear that they were two different things. The archetype itself was merely a predisposition to form images: "The archetype in itself is empty and purely formal, nothing but a *facultas praeformandi,* a possibility of representation which is given *a priori.*"[5] He also notes that it is the image that allows us to hypothesize the archetype: "One must constantly bear in mind that what we mean by 'archetype' is in itself irrepresentable, but that it has effects which enable us to visualize it, namely the archetypal image."[6] Even after 1946, Jung's justification for the theory of the collective unconscious remained confusing. He persisted in stating that the same images and themes are repeated in human history, resorting to the universality of the images as "proof" of the archetype at the same time that he denied claiming their universality.

In any case, the archetype (the structural component of the collective unconscious) is a hypothesis, and Jung recognized it as such. It is the assumption of a patterning process in the human brain, instinctual and alike everywhere, expressing itself in universal human behavior patterns, motifs, themes, images, and symbols. Jung sometimes likens the archetype itself to a vortex of energy, drawing to itself certain themes and images. Archetypal images, he noted, are accompanied by much emotion. They are those typically human experiences and accompanying images that touch us the most deeply. Because of their compelling quality, he also called them "numinous." Jung gave names to the most usual images. Shadow, anima and animus, child, trickster, and self are some of the best-known archetypal images, which we will discuss further below.

A bit of history will show Jung's "discovery" of the collective unconscious, its major component, the archetype, and the archetypal images. Jung's earliest work already showed his unusual respect for the unconscious. For example, in 1902, Jung wrote his doctoral dissertation, "On the Psychology and Pathology of So-called Occult Phenomena," on the subject of his young cousin, Helen Preiswerk, a medium. Jung called the medium's trance personalities "automatismes," meaning "autonomous" or "automatic personalities." He concluded his study by relating the origin of the unconscious, automatic personalities to the medium's own personality and psychological needs:

> They [repressed tendencies] are not lost; but as repressed thoughts analogous to the ideal of Ivenes [one of the automatic personalities], they begin to lead an independent existence as autonomous personalities.
>
> It is therefore conceivable that the phenomena of double consciousness are simply new character formations, or attempts of the future personality to break through.[7]

Jung's respect for these personalities presages his later view of the psyche as compensatory, by which he understands that whatever is missing from consciousness resides in the unconscious.

In Helen's case, the medium had so completely repressed the automatic personalities that they took on the characteristic of autonomy—they could act without the conscious knowledge of the medium herself. Jung spoke appreciatively of their "eminently teleological significance,"[8] meaning that these personalities contained an element missing in the medium's conscious personality and were therefore psychologically necessary, not to be dismissed as mere aberrations.

A similar perspective emerged in Jung's treatment of mental illness. In 1900, his decision to become a psychiatrist took him to the famous mental hospital in Zurich, the Burghölzli. There Jung pursued the symbolic meaning of his mental patients' "crazy" utterances with the same respect he had evidenced for the "automatic personalities" of his cousin. This was an unusual approach for his day, as it is for ours, and again it illustrates Jung's growing faith in the unconscious to provide what is missing in consciousness. If we cannot understand the message of the unconscious when it comes in "crazy" forms, Jung became convinced, that is because rational consciousness does not understand, or even tolerate, symbolism. His work with one patient, Babette, stands out. In this deeply disturbed woman, Jung found an autonomous complex (a voice) that made sense if interpreted symbolically. This voice even exhibited a sense of humor and irony.

> Once she said, with great emphasis, "I am the keystone, the monopoly of Schiller's *Bell,*" and the telephone [the dependable inner voice] remarked, "That is so important the markets will drop!" In all these examples the "telephone" has the character of an ironically commenting spectator who seems to be thoroughly convinced of the futility of these pathological fancies and mocks the patient's assertions in a superior tone.[9]

Jung's work with Babette, like that with the medium, fueled his growing conviction that the psyche operates on the principle of compensation. Dreams, fantasies, sand play, drawings, and even "nonsense" like Babette's can—if understood symbolically, not reductively—bring what is needed to consciousness. Jung came to consider every personality to be multiple, like the medium's and Babette's and like his own personalities number one and two. He came to take "automatic personalities," later called "complexes," even in normal people, very seriously. The difference between a "normal" personality and an "abnormal" one lay in the degree of the ego's awareness of the other personalities.

Jung assumed that the pre-individuated state was one of "contamination" of conscious and unconscious contents, or, as we said earlier, the state of being completely and unconsciously identified with a subpersonality. People in an unindividuated state either project the subpersonality onto others or are possessed by it (are totally compelled by its emotional quality). Neither state represents self-awareness. Individuation consists in coming to know the multiple personalities, the "little people" who dwell within one's breast. One needs to "befriend" them at the same time as one distinguishes one's own voice from theirs.[10] Although Jung described individuation as the process by which one becomes one's self, he did not mean this in a selfish, egocentric way. The self—the archetypal image that assumes nearly Godlike proportions—governs the whole process of individuation. Gradually the self displaces the ego as the center of consciousness.

Bear in mind the "automatic personalities" that Jung discovered in his cousin and the voice that made sense in the psychotic woman, Babette. These will help us understand more clearly what Jung means by a "complex" and an "archetypal image." Both the complex and the archetypal image can operate as an "autonomous subpersonality," although they are not identical. The difference between them is best understood in terms of each one's source. The complex has its origin in one's personal history, whereas the archetypal image has its origin in the collective unconscious. However, as Jung pointed out, every complex has an archetypal core. Edward Edinger, a Jungian analyst, defines the complex this way:

> A complex is an emotionally charged unconscious psychic entity made up of a number of associated ideas and images clustered around a central core [which is] an *archetypal image*. One recog-

nizes that a complex has been struck by the emergence of an affect which upsets psychic balance and disturbs the customary function of the ego.[11]

In common Jungian language, and in the popular culture, one might speak of a "mother complex" or a "father complex" in referring to an unhealed area of a person's psyche caused by early wounds in the relationship with the real mother or father. The complex would have an archetypal core, however, because while everyone has an individual mother and father, mother and father are universals and are fundamental to human existence. Mother and father images evoke all the energy and emotion that people everywhere feel about archetypal images.

Archetypal images, as distinguished from complexes, are common symbols, images, motifs, and themes portraying universal human experiences. Since symbols are archetypal images, they operate on the tension of opposites, which I explained in chapter 3 when discussing Jung's conflict model. As we know, Jung believed that without the energy generated by opposites, the psyche would not exist. Symbols, or archetypal images, both contain and transcend opposition, and this is what makes them so powerful. To illustrate what Jung means by this opposition, consider one of the most common archetypal images—the anima, a man's image of the feminine. In Jung's descriptions, the anima image exerts a powerful and ambivalent pull on men. Men's images of women range from the threatening seductress and the toothed vagina to the angelic and pure innocent. Men feel a deep ambivalence toward these images and, it seems, toward women themselves. This is an expression, Jung would say, of the polarity inherent in the images themselves. By definition, archetypal images contain, and at times transcend or unite, opposites.

A symbol can never be fully explained or understood rationally, which is why Jung preferred to amplify symbolic themes rather than pin them down with logic. Jung gave names to—personified—the most common archetypal images, among them, as we have seen, shadow, anima, animus, child, trickster, fool, Wise Old Man, Wise Old Woman, and the self. The self is the one archetypal image that specifically transcends oppositions, uniting them all. The energies of the archetypal images show up in dreams, fantasies, projections, and possessions. By giving names to them, one gains conscious access to the energy and emotions they contain.

Ego and persona are two components of every personality. They are primarily, though not entirely, conscious. Jung uses the term "complex" (e.g., "ego complex") to describe them, but here he means simply a constellation of images around a certain theme rather than the negative woundedness to which, for example, "mother complex" refers.

> By ego I understand a complex of ideas which constitutes the centre of my field of consciousness and appears to possess a high degree of continuity and identity. Hence I also speak of an *ego-complex*. The ego-complex is as much a content of my field of consciousness, . . . for a psychic element is conscious to me only in so far as it is related to my ego-complex. But inasmuch as the ego is only the centre of my field of consciousness, it is not identical with the totality of my psyche, being merely one complex among other complexes.[12]

Jung, like Freud, assumes that the ego is not really master in its own house. The prevalent opinion that it is, is an illusion. Its functioning can be disturbed by the intrusion of another complex from the unconscious. The psyche as a totality is actually "a contradictory multiplicity of complexes," of which the ego is one.[13] The ego does not usually know this until it runs up against an irresolvable conflict or other signs of neurosis. In this case, if a person seeks help from a Jungian, it is likely that the ego personality will become aware of the unconscious subpersonalities. In the individuation process, the ego must cede its place of centrality to the other "personalities," and this necessarily relativizes it.

The persona Jung likens to an actor's mask. Persona refers to the role one plays in society, and thus it is collective, not unique. It is not unimportant or superficial just because it is a "mask," but one needs to take care not to mistake the part one plays for one's identity. The persona, Jung said, "feigns individuality, making others and oneself believe that one is individual, whereas one is simply acting a role through which the collective psyche speaks."[14] "Every calling, or profession, for example, has its own characteristic persona. . . . Only, the danger is that [people] become identical with their personas—the professor with his text-book, the tenor with his voice." [15] Although not so usual as having an overdeveloped persona, some people have inadequate personas—that is, they do not know how to act in social situations. In such a case, a Jungian analyst would help the person develop a stronger persona. Doing so might feel inauthentic, like learning to "play a role," to the person in question, but if one cannot perform a social role then one will suffer. Since Jung assumes that people often begin with a good, even too good, adaptation to social necessities, one is practically bound to stumble, in the course of individuation, upon elements not included in one's social role—even elements that are directly antithetical to the persona. The persona is compensatory to both the shadow and the anima (or the animus, if one is a woman): "The persona, the ideal picture of a man as he should be, is inwardly compensated by feminine weakness." [16] Edward Whitmont describes the relationship most succinctly: "The brighter the persona, the darker the shadow." [17]

Projection of and possession by complexes and archetypal images are the two typical ways humans experience the autonomous personalities before coming to know and being able to integrate them. Projection is the perceptual "trick" by which we perceive in others what are actually characteristics in ourselves. That does not mean that the person on whom we project the qualities does not have them. He or she probably "has a hook out for the projection," as Jungians say, or we would not project the qualities on them in the first place. However, when projection is operating, we overreact to the qualities we see in the other, negatively or positively. The degree of emotion we feel about the other person is a clue as to whether or not we are projecting. During the course of individuation, one withdraws projections. This means not only that one projects less on other people, but also that one's own personality is enlarged by the acceptance of qualities that were previously denied, projected onto others.

Possession, on the other hand, means being taken over by a "subpersonality" of which one is unaware, "acting out" in its voice without consciously choosing to do so and without knowing that one is doing it. Possession can make people act in ways their conscious sense of themselves would never permit. For example, a docile person who was never allowed to express anger and therefore repressed all angry feelings could, on occasion, be "possessed" by her angry subpersonality and say and do things that her sweet self could not allow. Projection and possession occur because of the ego's exclusion of the unconscious qualities. The more "unconscious" one is, the more exaggerated the "trick" perception, via projection or possession, tends to be.

A well-known Jungian method for promoting acquaintance between the multiple selves is "dialogue with the unconscious." By this Jung means carrying on a conversation with an inner figure (a dream or fantasy figure, for instance) by suspending rational judgment, getting back into the mood of the dream or fantasy, and inviting the dream or fantasy figure to speak. The figure will speak back exactly as if it were another person. Even though the "dialogue" is intrapsychic rather than interpersonal, it is real. Jung's method of personification is highly imaginative, with each "little person" in the psyche, including the ego, engaged in conversation with the others. Dialoguing with the "little people" in the psyche generates self-acceptance, as one learns to treat them as if they had a right to live. The ego sheds its usual harshness and its monolithic perspective and thus is transformed as well as relativized when it engages in "dialogue" with archetypal images such as the shadow, anima, or animus. Increased gentleness toward oneself—one's inner cast of characters—can be transformative in itself. Theoretically, as a result of becoming gentler and more accepting toward ourselves, we become less judgmental and tyrannical toward others. Possibilities of projection and possession lessen.

Neurosis, in Jung's terms, is a split, a "cleavage" within oneself, and the split is between conscious and unconscious. Archetypal images may play a central or a peripheral part in neurosis, but usually the personal unconscious with its "complexes" is more prominent. People experience neurosis under many guises in their lives, perhaps as a relationship conflict, or as depression, or as inability to work. Possession and projection can play their part in neurosis too. A person may experience a neurotic problem as "out there" rather than "in here." When willpower is not sufficient to resolve such problems, Jung would assume the presence of a neurosis. The powerlessness a person feels before a neurosis (the fact that willpower is of no avail) is proof for Jung that half of the conflict is unconscious. Jungian analysis provides the opportunity to uncover the unconscious roots of the neurosis, to work through the symbolic meaning of the conflict, and to release the energy that has been bound up in it. People often come into analysis because of neurosis. It has a positive side therefore, since, propelled by the pain it causes, a person may be forced into individuation, which is the task of life.

Jung implicitly criticizes Western, rational, technological society in his theory of the individuation process and in his definition of neurosis. For example, he observed that socialization in Western society forces almost everyone into extraversion, even though not all people are natural extraverts. To be accepted in Western society, people must engage in frequent interaction with others and constant busyness. Little time is afforded for reflection, and those who choose a reflective life style are likely to be misunderstood and undervalued. Introverts—those who prefer solitude and take their bearings from their own inner feelings—may indeed become "successful extraverts," but they do damage to their own natures that way. This is one of many possible causes of neurosis—being shaped by society's predilections into a person one is not. In the above case, the repressed and necessary introversion is in the unconscious. Jung's is ultimately a teleological vision of the unconscious, since the seeds of health and wholeness reside there. This emphasis sets him apart from Freud.

Usually the first of one's "inner cast of characters" encountered in individuation is the shadow—the name Jung gave to the "negative," often despised and repressed side of the personality. Since it takes the form of the "opposite" of the conscious personality, it includes the inferior functions and attitude of the particular type as well as other qualities consciousness rejects. Jung describes it as both a complex and an archetypal image. He felt that in the course of individuation a person usually encounters the shadow before other archetypal images because it primarily comprises factors in the personal unconscious rather than the collective unconscious, although it has elements of both. The shadow is therefore closer to consciousness and easier to come to know. I will elaborate on the shadow at some length because I believe this concept to be an extremely important one, both to individuals and, as we shall see, to nations.

Jung believed that we experience the shadow in others of the same sex, projecting shadow qualities onto a woman if we are women and onto a man if we are men. The shadow, being the opposite of one's conscious personality, is usually experienced as negative, at least until it is integrated (known, accepted, and transformed). The shadow is not always felt as negative, however, because, like all archetypal images, it exists on the principle of tension of opposites, having a positive and a negative pole. A person could repress, even despise, "light" or good qualities, in which case the shadow would contain them. More often, however, the shadow contains the "dark" qualities because our upbringing causes us to reject them. Christianity, as well as other religions, associates "dark qualities" with evil, and we are taught to despise them. Jung was harshly critical of what he saw as the Christian ideal of perfection. He believed that this ideal was both impossible to attain and responsible for the harsh repressiveness with which we treat ourselves and others. Christian perfectionism is a main factor in the creation of our individual shadows. Having been brought up to deny anger, greed, envy, sexual desires, and the like, where do those feelings go? Into the shadow, claims Jung.

Jung believes that we need to assimilate the autonomous personalities consciously. The integrated shadow offers substance to the conscious personality. Let us take our example of the docile woman who never permits herself anger. She experiences another woman as angry and hates the anger in the other woman, denouncing her and focusing on her to the point of obsession. This is a shadow projection. Jung's method of treatment would invove the patient's looking within herself to discover whether she has any of the anger, or envy of the freedom that anger represents and that she hates in the other person. This looking within has to be more than an intellectual act, since the ego-consciousness that analyzes is hostile to the shadow. Jung would encourage this patient to let her feeling toward the angry woman emerge fully—not to act upon it, but to acknowledge and feel it consciously. She would probably feel contempt, irritation, and anger toward the angry woman. Allowing her repressed feelings into the open can be cathartic in itself, causing her to hate the angry woman less and even to feel a measure of compassion for her. This would involve withdrawing the projection and beginning to acknowledge her own capacity for anger.

In the end, the anger she has repressed could add forcefulness to her overly docile personality. This change would be, in Jung's terms, the shadow's "substance" added to her conscious sense of herself. She would now "cast a shadow."

Jung's discussions of the shadow link it with the problem of evil:

> What seems evil, or at least meaningless and valueless to contemporary experience and knowledge, might on a higher level of experience and knowledge appear as the source of the best—everything depending, naturally, on the use one makes of one's seven devils. To explain them as meaningless robs the personality of its proper shadow, and without this it loses its form. The living form needs deep shadow if it is not to appear plastic. Without shadow it remains a two-dimensional phantom, a more or less well brought-up child.[18]

For Jung, the unintegrated shadow represents a moral problem, although integrated, it represents the possibility of greater wholeness. Coming to terms with it therefore constitutes nearly a moral imperative. On no other subject does Jung adopt such a prophetic tone. Inasmuch as the shadow is related to the problem of evil, Jung's vision has a positive twist to it, because by acknowledging and integrating what the ego conceives of as "evil"—most often found in the shadow—one prevents the shadow, as autonomous subpersonality, from continuing to act out blindly. Personal "evil" can be transformed.

Particularly important is Jung's extension of the shadow theory into the relations of nations with one another. Nations have what Jung called a "collective shadow" that they project onto other nations. Like individuals, they perceive what their own nation has repressed as evil in another nation. In this way, seeds of irresolvable conflict and war are planted. Each nation needs to withdraw the projection and come to terms with its own shadow, in order for the international situation to improve. The United States and the Soviet Union are indulging in mutual shadow projection when each sees itself as morally pure and perceives the other as evil and imperialistic. The United States vaunts itself as a "Christian nation," while the Communists are castigated as atheists. The Soviet Communists believe their society is more moral than ours because theirs provides for the needs of all the people. They criticize us for our environmental pollution and the enormous gap between the rich and the poor perpetuated by the luxury items that the wealthy purchase. There may indeed be some truth in each nation's critical perception of the other, but the emotional obsession and the self-righteous quality of the criticism suggest shadow involvement. Because of this, the argument does not advance beyond mutual vilification.

> And just as the typical neurotic is unconscious of his *shadow side,* so the normal individual, like the neurotic, sees his shadow in his neighbor or in the man beyond the great divide. It has even become a political and social duty to apostrophize the capitalism of the one and the communism of the other as the very devil, so as to fascinate the outward eye and prevent it from looking at the individual life within.[19]

At least as frightening and dangerous as national shadow projection is the possibility of mass shadow possession. Hitler's hypnotic power over many people is often cited as an example. Being possessed by the shadow means being taken over by it, without one's conscious knowledge. In Hitler's case, as with lesser shadow possessions, the conscious personality rationalizes what the shadow does in the name of good, since the shadow is, by definition, opposed to the conscious personality's view of itself. In a shadow possession, the ego-ideal is mesmerized into the shadow's point of view. Hitler spoke with the power of the unintegrated shadow, touching deeply upon other people's unconscious hatred and fear, causing them to accept the rationalization for the shadow's behavior. The shadow, like all archetypal images that are unintegrated, is hypnotic, compelling, spellbinding. Hitler's racism, fanaticism, excessive scrupulosity, and desire for "purity" are all good examples of the self-deception of the unintegrated, archetypal shadow. They also bear out Jung's thesis that unconsciousness itself is evil. Lack of awareness of one's own unconscious leaves one at its mercy.

Transformation of the personal shadow is possible, however. First the shadow must be recognized—either through the full and conscious expression of its feelings or through personification—so that the ego can dialogue with it. The evil that the shadow caused before integration can be transformed in the encounter with the ego. Like two opposing personalities, the two can learn to get along with one another. The integration of the shadow is humbling, especially if one's ego-ideal is harshly perfectionistic. "Befriended," however, the shadow can become an ally to the ego.

Although the shadow is relatively free of sexist overtones, it is not free of racist ones. Jung often called the shadow the "dark side" or the "black side" of the personality and sometimes went so far as to liken the shadow to a black-skinned person: "This figure often appears as dark-skinned and of mongoloid type, and then it represents a negative and possibly dangerous aspect. Sometimes it can hardly be distinguished, if at all, from the shadow."[20] Obviously this description would not work for a black person since the shadow is the opposite of the conscious personality. Even though the point of the shadow theory was to integrate the so-called "dark side," Jung's theory was "white-centric" as well as androcentric.

Under Jung's schema, acquaintance with one's anima or animus usually comes after integration of the shadow. As we have seen, anima is the image of the female in a man's unconscious and animus is the image (or images) of the male in a woman's unconscious. Jung designates these inner figures as "archetypal images" more often than as "complexes," although he refers to them by both names. He sees them as stemming more from the collective unconscious, and less from the personal unconscious, than does the shadow. They are not completely assimilable for this reason. Like all complexes and archetypal images prior to their integration, anima and animus can either possess a person or be projected. To achieve wholeness, people need the perspective of the anima or animus in the same way that they need the shadow. Integration of the contrasexual image expands and broadens the personality, giving it access to qualities thought to belong to the other sex.

Anima and animus are both archetypal and personal. Individuals' anima or animus images are constructed, in part, on their experience of the opposite sex—especially in early life. The earlier the experience occurs, the more influence it has on the contrasexual image and the more likely that it will become part of the personal unconscious (rather than remaining conscious). However, since anima and animus are archetypal, they draw their power from a much deeper source than the personal unconscious. Jung posited a threefold source for anima and animus: (1) personal experience; (2) an innate, unconscious, genetically based contrasexuality in each person—an a priori category—or, as he also put it, a predisposition for imaging contrasexually (an archetype); (3) a collective, inherited image of the opposite sex, transmitted through mythology, fairy tales, art history, religious history (archetypal image).

Of the inherited image, Jung had this to say:

> It seems to me, therefore, that apart from the influence of woman there is also the man's own femininity to explain the feminine nature of the soul-complex. . . . We have, in this matter, the testimony of art from all ages, and besides that, the famous question: *habet mulier animam?* [Does woman have a soul?] [21]

Jung felt that men's images of the soul were feminine and projected onto women. He found corroboration for his theory in religious art from all ages and from his own experience and that of his patients. In contrast, Jung translates animus as "spirit," Logos, power of the word. Since he observed that men lack Eros (relatedness, or what he called "soul") and women lack Logos (access to the spirit, the intellect), both anima and animus compensate for what is lacking to consciousness. Because anima means "soul," and because women have an animus, not an anima, Jung frequently repeated the old Church conundrum as to whether or not women have souls. This seems a strange and oblique question for him to pursue. I wonder if he found it amusing or ironic, or if he thought it had real merit. Even while raising this issue about women's souls, Jung explained that his concept of the male "soul" was not a theological one. His term "anima" was meant psychologically, erotically. However, he turned to theology for justification of his question about women's souls, and in so doing, he resurrected an old theological concern that was blind with misogyny.

Naomi Goldenberg brought the derivative and problematic quality of Jung's concept of the animus to public attention. She directs us to the following quotation from Jung: "Since the anima is an archetype that is found in men, it is reasonable to suppose that an equivalent archetype must be present in women; for just as the man is compensated by a feminine element, so woman is compensated by a masculine one." Jung tries to qualify the statement: "I do not, however, wish to give the impression that these compensatory relationships were arrived at by deduction. On the contrary, long and varied experience was needed in order to grasp the nature of the anima and animus empirically." [22] Jung did note, however, that women often have difficulty understanding what the animus is:

> So far as my experience goes, a man always understands fairly easily what is meant by the anima; indeed, as I said, he frequently has a quite definite picture of her, so that from a varied collection of women of all periods he can single out the one who comes closest to the anima-type. But I have, as a rule, found it very difficult to make a woman understand what the animus is, and I have never met any woman who could tell me anything definite about his personality. [23]

Perhaps Jung's apparent doubt about the female soul, as well as his hypothetical derivation of the animus (it did not arise out of women's experience), explains women's difficulty in understanding what it is that he means by animus.

Projection of and possession by these contrasexual "personalities" have unique qualities. Projection of the contrasexual archetypal images is usually experienced as falling in love, with the prerequisite of someday withdrawing the projection. Possession by the contrasexual personality has its own typical characteristics. As the anima is a man's unconscious image of the female, it can function in him as an "inferior" feminine personality. Thus if a man is possessed by his anima, he acts like an "inferior woman." (All these terms are Jung's.) This would involve his acting in ways that are stereotypically permitted to women but not to men, such as crying, being sullen, sulky, tearful, plaintive, or otherwise emotional. Jung felt that when a man is possessed by his anima, he is not in control of his emotions; he is completely taken over by them. A woman, on the other hand, when possessed by her animus will act like an "inferior man." That means, for Jung, that she will insist, shrilly, on the rightness of her opinions. Not being at home in the male world of logic and facts, when she does enter this territory she does it ineptly. The man is similarly inept in the world of emotion. An anima-possessed man is "moody," while an "animus-possessed" woman is "bitchy." These two "complexes" often touch each other off, and typical descriptions of this anima-animus interaction have the woman nagging and the man cowering. We will discuss the "animus-possessed" woman at length in my feminist critique in chapter 6.

Like the shadow, the unintegrated anima and animus tend to have the characteristics of the inferior function. For example, if a man is primarily a "thinking type," his anima will be a "feeling type." Projection will involve falling in love with "feeling type" women, who "carry" the feeling function for him as long as possible. When he is possessed by his anima, he is in the grips of "inferior feeling." Finally, integration of the anima will give him access to feeling. This is the typical configuration reinforced by our society. It gets tricky if one considers that a man could be a "feeling type" himself, which would make his anima a "thinking type," for then she would lead him into clear and focused thinking—an inconsistency not worked through in the theory, since anima integration is always the integration of soul, feeling, and relatedness. The case of the animus is parallel. If a woman is primarily a "feeling type," her animus figures will be "thinking types," which she will project onto men. To be possessed by the animus is to be in the grip of inferior thinking, and integration of the animus implies that a woman can integrate, use gracefully, her thinking function. Here again, if the person's typology does not match patriarchal society's preferred female and male types, the descriptions break down.

Integration of the contrasexual image gives men and women access to qualities that are seen as belonging to the other sex. Jung often described anima and animus as "gateways to the unconscious." The anima was supposed to lead men into the depths, as Beatrice led Dante or as Salome, the young female image he encountered during his "confrontation with the unconscious," instructed Jung. Jung frequently refers to the anima as "she," illustrating with this language the autonomy with which he endowed this image, reminiscent of the "automatic personalities" in his early works. The anima appears to men as a real woman, or as images of women in men's dreams and fantasies. "She" is the psychic entity that seduces, lures, attracts, and even imperils a man. "She" compels him to enter the unconscious. "She" also leads him into unexplored depths of feeling, relationship, and sensitivity when he allows "her" to do so. The animus functions on the same principle. "He" (or "they," since, as we shall see below, the animus is conceived of as plural) provides a guiding light, an ability to focus, a clarity of thought, precision, and analytical ability for a woman. The integrated animus leads a woman into the world of the spirit, erudition, and the power of the word.

Jung explains the plurality of the animus, as contrasted with the singular nature of the anima, on the principle of compensation. "Consciously," that is, in his "outer life," a man has multiple relationships with women. Therefore, in the unconscious, one primary feminine image holds sway. The reverse holds for a woman. "Consciously," as Jungians call it, or in "the world," she is likely to be monogamous. Therefore, in her unconscious are multiple animus figures. In both cases, the unconscious is compensatory for the life lived, with a man's longings focused on the single anima image, and a woman's longings on multiple male images. This particular ramification of the balance model clearly lends archetypal legitimation to an unequal social situation between the sexes.

We see Jung's assumption of a natural balance in all of these descriptions. The idea of balance predominates in several ways: the most obvious is that what is lacking in the conscious personality is provided by the unconscious. With the ideas of opposition, compensation, and balance as governing paradigms, Jung and Jungians have tended to downplay the necessary imbalance between the anima and animus in a culture that devalues women. However, they have not ignored this dimension entirely. Jolande Jacobi, for example, in her discussion of women's psychology and the power of the animus recognizes the imprint of patriarchy on these images: "For in consequence of the patriarchally oriented development of our Western culture, the woman too tends to think that the masculine as such is more valuable than the feminine, and this attitude does much to increase the power of the animus." However, she fails to pursue this insight, reverting to the nature argument as she continues her discussion: "But just as the male by his very nature is uncertain in the realm of Eros, so the woman will always be insecure in the realm of Logos. What woman has to overcome in respect to the animus is not pride but inertia and lack of self-confidence." [24] Is a woman, then, naturally lacking in self-confidence in the realm of Logos? Does she have a natural inertia? Jacobi has backed away from the implications of her insight about the consequences of our patriarchal culture on women's development by appealing to the law of nature. Her explanation of women's inertia and lack of self-confidence would have been more consistent had she stuck to her earlier insight about the consequences of Western patriarchy.

In fact we can go further, and consider that to construct a theory on the illusion of balance functions to mask the gender imbalance that exists in patriarchy. If in our society psychological and social symmetry between the sexes were the fact, then to actualize the "other side" of the psyche would be appropriate. Since, however, we live in a radically asymmetrical social and gender situation, to pursue the illusion of balance as the goal of life is to avoid and thereby legitimate the social problem of inequality between the sexes.

During individuation, both gaining distance from and incorporating the viewpoints of anima and animus are central achievements. The point of individuation, ultimately, is to become one's self. Interestingly, Jung speaks of the "self" one "becomes" as an archetypal image as well. Actually, since the self is an archetypal image—the image governing the entire process—one does not so much "become" it as one allows it to manifest itself. Jung calls the self both the "mid-point of the psyche," meaning that it is "midway between the conscious and unconscious," and the archetypal image of totality embracing the whole psyche. He also describes it as the "center and circumference of the psyche." This kind of language is decidedly religious:

> I have called this centre the *self*. Intellectually the self is no more than a psychological concept, a construct that serves to express the unknowable essence which we cannot grasp as such, since by definition it transcends our powers of comprehension. It might equally well be called the "God within us." The beginnings of our whole psychic life seem to be inextricably rooted in this point, and all our highest and ultimate purposes seem to be striving towards it. This paradox is unavoidable, as always, when we try to define something that lies beyond the bourn of our understanding.[25]

Jung distinguishes the ego from the self, revealing, again, the self's religious nature, and, as James Hillman points out, Jung's ultimately monotheistic stance. Going beyond the necessarily limited perspective of the ego is reminiscent of the goal of both Eastern and Western religions: "The ego is only the subject of my consciousness, while the self is the subject of my total psyche, which also includes the unconscious." [26]

In *Aion*, Jung describes the archetypal image of the self as including all of the other ones. He again likens the self to the image of God: "Unity and totality stand at the highest point on the scale of objective values because their symbols can no longer be distinguished from the *imago Dei*." [27] Symbols of the self (and correspondingly, of God) range from a quaternity, mandala, flower, trees, mountains, lakes, serpents, birds, elephants, and horses to the Wise Old Man, Wise Old Woman, the Rex and Regina of alchemy, and the Christ. The Christ seems to be and yet not to be a symbol of the self for Jung. Essentially, Jung felt that Christ lacked the dimension of evil and thus could not be a complete self symbol. Sometimes Jung linked the Christ and the Antichrist together for a complete symbol, since the self is a *complexio,* or *coniunctio, oppositorum.*

> In the empirical self, light and shadow form a paradoxical unity. In the Christian concept, on the other hand, the archetype is hopelessly split into two irreconcilable halves, leading ultimately to a metaphysical dualism—the final separation of the kingdom of heaven from the fiery world of the damned. . . . Psychologically, the case is clear, since the dogmatic figure of Christ is so sublime and spotless that everything else turns dark beside it. It is, in fact, so one-sidedly perfect that it demands a psychic complement to restore the balance. [28]

Jung explains the nature of the *coniunctio* most fully in an essay entitled "The Psychology of the Transference." Here he compares the practice of alchemy in the sixteenth century to the discoveries of analytical psychology in the twentieth. He alludes to similar parallels in Gnosticism and other "unorthodox" branches of Christianity. The central process of alchemy was the transformation of base elements into gold, a process Jung believed was analogous to the transformation that occurs during individuation. He likened the transference between analyst and patient to the *coniunctio* (more specifically to the sacred marriage and the *hierosgamos*) that took place between the King and Queen in alchemy. (The King and Queen, also symbolized by the Sun and Moon, are central alchemical images that Jung took to be portrayals of the self.) "The important part played in the history of alchemy by the *hierosgamos* and the mystical marriage, and also by the conjunction, correspond to the central significance of the transference in psychotherapy on the one hand and in the field of normal human relationships on the other."[29]

The crux of this essay lies in the central importance of the *coniunctio*—the immersion together of the King and Queen in the bath during the act of coitus. Jung understood this act to represent the coming together of opposites, an act enormously significant in the soul-making process. This coming together is so powerful that the death of the royal pair is the immediate result. Jung likens this to the death of the ego during individuation, after which the birth of the self can result. Freud has often been criticized for sexualizing spirituality. Here in the highly erotic descriptions of the act of intercourse between the King and Queen, Jung can be seen to be doing just the opposite, spiritualizing sexuality. Jung's choice of powerful sexual imagery for this central process—"constellated" during therapy in the transference between the analyst and the patient—with no acknowledgment or discussion of explicit sexual overtones, leaves in question whether or not he believes that sexual intercourse between analyst and analysand is appropriate. Jung's account of this transference phenomenon are highly ambiguous, suggesting most of the time an intrapsychic process, and yet at others, an interpersonal one:

> The main fact is the *subjective experience* of the situation—in other words, it is a mistake to believe that one's personal dealings with one's partner play the most important part. . . . Nor does the *coniunctio* take place with the personal partner; it is a royal game played out between the active, masculine side of the woman (the animus) and the passive, feminine side of the man (the anima). Although the two figures are always tempting the ego to identify itself with them, a real understanding even on the personal level is possible only if the identification is refused. Non-identification demands considerable moral effort. . . . The personal protagonists in the royal game should constantly bear in mind that at bottom it represents the "trans-subjective" union of archetypal figures, and it should never be forgotten that it is a *symbolical* relationship whose goal is complete individuation.[30]

Having apparently established the *coniunctio* within the intra-psychic dynamic, Jung suggests that what one does about the transference at this stage represents a difficult moral problem. His language implies that the erotic element becomes so strong that a difficult choice must be made, and that neither alternative is completely right. He does not spell out what the choice involves: "The right way, like the wrong way, must be paid for." Individuation requires, Jung says, an *opus contra naturam,* a work against nature. As he says, "It goes against nature to commit incest and it goes against nature not to yield to an ardent desire." [31] To what moral conflict is Jung referring? Does he really mean that the desire for sex between the (usually male) analyst and the (usually female) patient becomes so intense that a decision either way is "against nature"? From that point, Jung continues to discuss the conflict in spiritualized and intra-psychic terms: "Whenever this drive for wholeness appears, it begins by disguising itself under the symbolism of incest." [32]

The next step in individuation is the near-death of the ego: "The personality becomes so vastly enlarged that the normal ego-personality is almost extinguished." [33] After that, either a positive or a negative inflation of the ego occurs. Jung likens positive inflation to megalomania and negative inflation to annihilation of the ego. In either case, a new configuration can now be born, which Jung calls a "natural symbol," the self. He also calls it a "supraordinate personality." "This almighty taskmaster is none other than the self. The self wants to be made manifest in the work, and for this reason the *opus* is a process of individuation, a becoming of the self." [34]

Note the centrality of sexual symbolism to this birth of the self. Gay students in classes where I have taught Jungian psychology have noted the heterosexism in this model, wondering if and how this central aspect of individuation applies to them. Other implications of the discussion of transference concern me as well. We now know that Jung was involved romantically with at least two of his female clients, Sabina Spielrein and Toni Wolff. We also know that the relationship between Wolff and Jung was long-lasting and sexual. I pass no judgment about the quality of their relationship. My point is that knowledge of these two analytic relationships adds weight to the suspicion that Jung is indeed referring in his symbolism to the desire for sexual intimacy between analyst and patient. Given the context in which we live—particularly now that we know how often analysts have engaged in sexual relations with their patients—it seems to me that guidelines are necessary. Besides leaving the question of sex between analyst and analysand open, Jung's romantic discussion of the *coniunctio* in alchemy, and his likening of its central process to the transference in analysis, omits consideration of the power differential between analyst and analysand. If a male analyst has intercourse, or even engages in flirtation, with a female patient, he will be playing into her social conditioning to find her worth in her attractiveness to a man. This confirmation of her sexual attractiveness will not help her emerge to full personhood, since any therapy that does not challenge internalized oppression in a woman is not a freeing therapy for her.

What Jung intends is that the drive toward wholeness consists in uniting the "masculine" and "feminine" sides of the personality. Following the process through, a new state is achieved. As in our previous discussion of the tension between "conflict" language and "harmony" language in Jung's psychological models, here we find an unresolved ambiguity between "self as a state" and "self as a process." At times Jung describes the self as our life's "goal," which lends weight to the "self as state" reading: "The self could be characterized as a kind of compensation of the conflict between inside and outside. This formulation would not be unfitting, since the self has somewhat the character of a result, of a goal attained, something that has come to pass very gradually and is experienced with much travail." [35] This reading is counterbalanced by other statements in which Jung emphasizes that the contradiction of life is never resolved once and for all: "[The opposites and contradictions] constantly threaten the unity of the personality and entangle life again and again in their dichotomies." [36] Perhaps even more suggestive of a "process" or "dynamic" reading of the self is the following: "We are dealing here with very important 'nuclear processes' in the objective psyche—'*images of the goal*,' as it were, which the psychic process, being goal-directed, apparently sets up of its own accord, without any external stimulus." [37] If, in fact, Jung equates the self with God (which he certainly comes close to doing, even if not consistently or theo-logically), it would seem that the self can no more be "attained" than God can. The "dynamic" reading would thus seem more appropriate.

In the preceding discussion of the archetypal image of the self, Jung's language is metaphorical, suggestive, and religious. Yet he understood his "map of the psyche" to be objective, em-pirical, and scientific. Indeed, Jung took great pains to defend the empirical nature of analytical psychology. In the beginning of *Psychology and Religion: West and East,* he states: "Although I have often been called a philosopher, I am an empiricist and adhere as such to the phenomenological standpoint."[38]

By calling himself an empiricist, Jung distinguished himself from philosophers and theologians and situated his work in the natural sciences. "From a philosophical standpoint my em-pirical concepts would be logical monsters, and as a philosopher I should cut a very sorry figure indeed."[39] Commenting further on his method, Jung says: "This standpoint is exclusively phe-nomenological, that is, it is concerned with occurrences, events, experiences—in a word, with facts."[40] Yet what Jung means by "facts" departs from the agreed-upon definition. Speaking of himself as a scientist, Jung says that his "primary interest is the verification of psychic facts."[41] The word "psy-chic" would seem to remove the "facts" from the material level of observable data. For Jung, however, no contradiction exists between "psychic" and "facts." Psyche is the realm of the real: "We might well say, on the contrary, that physical existence is a mere inference, since we know of matter only in so far as we perceive psychic images mediated by the senses. . . . Not only does the psyche exist, it is existence itself."[42]

What exactly, then, did Jung mean by his "empiricism"? Critics frequently chastised him for not being empirical, and he refuted the charge again and again. He often cited as example his word-association test, which was the most experimental, repeatable, and verifiable work he had done. But then he would switch the level of the discussion on his critics by talking about "psychic facts," thus confirming their skepticism. Actually, however, Jung was an empiricist in the two usual senses of the word. He had based his early works on observation and experi-ment (the word-association test and experimental work with mental patients) as well as on his own experience. But Jung's later method was phenomenological. He amassed enormous quantities of data—numerous dreams, for example—and then compared them, finding universal themes and motifs. From there, he constructed his model, the archetype.

As confusing as all that is, it is not as as anti science as it may seem on the surface. Ian Barbour, in his discussion of methods in science, points out that the inductive ideal (generalizing from the particular, supposedly in keeping with the data) is an unsatisfactory account of what scientists actually do.

> The mere amassing of data or cataloguing of facts does not produce a scientific theory. . . . Theoretical terms are *mental constructs* which may be suggested by the data but are never given to us directly by nature. They have a status logically different from that of the data, and hence offer a type of explanation that no mere summary of the data could achieve. The empiricist tradition has never adequately represented the role of concepts and theories in science.[43]

Jung's understanding of science was very similar to Barbour's: "I trust that it does not conflict with the principles of scientific empiricism if one occasionally makes certain reflections which go beyond a mere accumulation and classification of experience."[44] While Jung frequently defended his methodology as a phenomenologist and an empiricist (against the accusation that he was a mystic and an obscurantist), he was aware of the limitations of empiricism as it is usually understood. In true scientific spirit, Jung was ready to put his theoretical constructs behind him whenever a better expression came along.

> Psychology, like every empirical science, cannot get along without auxiliary concepts, hypotheses, and models. But the theologian as well as the philosopher is apt to make the mistake of taking them for metaphysical postulates. The atom of which the physicist speaks is not an *hypostasis,* it is a *model.* Similarly, my concept of the archetype or of psychic energy is only an auxiliary idea which can be exchanged at any time for a better formula.[45]

Jung's work stands at the intersection of religion and science. Any boundary work is liable to criticism from both sides, seeming to each to belong to the other and claimed by neither. In the final analysis, and especially in his later years, it seems to me that Jung deliberately went beyond the limits of the empirical viewpoint that he had so ardently defended earlier. This is evident in a late statement about the self:

> It seems to me that our psychological inquiry must come to a stop here, for the idea of a self is itself a transcendental postulate which, although justifiable psychologically, does not allow of scientific proof. This step beyond science is an unconditional requirement of the psychological development I have sought to depict, because without this postulate I could give no adequate formulation of the psychic processes that occur empirically.[46]

From a feminist perspective, both Jung's religious stance and his adherence to scientific principles of inquiry merit questioning because unconscious gender assumptions creep into both religion and science. Patriarchal religion has been accepted as transcendent and revealed, and thus as above human criticism. Patriarchal science has stood on the principle of empirical investigation, without scientists' awareness of the possibility of gender assumptions influencing the choice of data, the method of investigation, and the results. Because Jung's psychology partakes of the status of both religion and psychology, even though it also suffers loss of credibility by being associated with both, his pronouncements about the nature of the "feminine" and women can stand on practically unassailable grounds—"sacred" on the one hand, and "empirical" on the other.

In the next chapter we will examine the religious nature of Jung's psychology in more depth. This examination is not intended to "debunk" his work because of its religious nature. On the contrary, its spiritual depth is one of its strongest drawing cards. My intent is to draw out more clearly the religious nature of Jung's psychology, so that we can see the sacred underpinnings and hence what makes some of his assumptions about women above criticism.

5

EXPERIENCE IS SACRED: JUNG'S PSYCHOLOGY AS RELIGION

Scholars have long noted the religious nature of Jung's psychology. Theologians, mainly, but not all, Christian, have wrestled hard with Jung. Their responses to him follow the typical lines of polarization, from the wholly approving to the harshly skeptical. Clifford A. Brown remarks that the critics, while varying widely in their assessments, all indict Jung for overstepping epistemological boundaries between theology and psychology. [1] These critics range from the Catholic father Victor White— originally accepting, but later disapproving—to the renowned Jewish theologian and philosopher Martin Buber. All focus on Jung's "God-talk" (language about God), taking him to task for what they see as his opportunistic recourse to Kantian epistemology—his use of Kant when it suits him to "justify" his psychology philosophically and his disregard of the boundaries of philosophy on the whole. We, too, will focus on Jung's "God-talk," for it provides a unique pathway into the heart of his psychology and his psychoreligious dilemma.

Throughout his writings, Jung scattered appreciative references to the work of Immanuel Kant. In particular, he drew on Kant for confirmation of his central idea, the archetype, and especially the God-archetype. Jung's references to Kant nearly always involve an attempt to stave off misunderstandings of his own work as "metaphysical." He consistently rejected any association with the metaphysical, stating repeatedly that his standpoint was psychological and empirical.

> The fact that I am content with what can be experienced psychically, and reject the metaphysical, does not amount, as any intelligent person can see, to a gesture of skepticism or agnosticism aimed at faith and trust in higher powers, but means approximately the same as what Kant meant when he called the thing-in-itself a "merely negative borderline concept." Every statement about the transcendental is to be avoided because it is only a laughable presumption on the part of a human mind unconscious of its limitations.[2]

James Heisig notes that "Kant had already demonstrated, at least to Jung's satisfaction, that 'there can be no empirical knowledge that is not already caught and limited by the *a priori* structure of cognition.'"[3] Kant's demonstration seemed to Jung to pave the way for his own concept of an inherited, collective, psychic structure that "conditions all experience, conscious and unconscious."[4] Jung consistently drew on Kant for his insistence on the primacy of the image, rather than of the "thing-in-itself," and it is clear that he was willing to stretch to the limit the analogy between his own work and that of Kant: "The archetype would thus be, to borrow from Kant, the noumenon of the image which intuition perceives and, in perceiving, creates."[5] We will see in Jung's "God-talk" further evidence of his willingness to appropriate Kant's carefully worked-out philosophical categories for justification of his own ideas. Jung's use of Kant frustrated his critics, especially in the light of his frequent rejection of any association with philosophy.

One of the most thoughtful critics of Jung is Martin Buber, whose argument hinges on Jung's "Kantian epistemology" in a particular way: he faults Jung for collapsing the distinction between the psychic and the religious. Since Jung concentrates so heavily on the image, refusing to say anything about the metaphysical, Buber feels that he has thereby proclaimed the "religion of psychic immanence," confusing psychology with religion. For Buber, if Jung's "God" is nothing but an archetype in the collective unconscious, then Jung has obliterated a fundamental aspect of God, his Otherness. While Buber's God is both transcendent and immanent, to lose the one for the other is to lose God.[6] Jung's psychology itself is a new religion, claims Buber: "In short, although the new psychology protests that it is 'no world-view but a science,' it no longer contents itself with the role of an interpreter of religion. It proclaims the new religion, the only one which can still be true, the religion of pure psychic immanence."[7] Buber's claim that Jung's psychology is a religion can be well supported, I believe, although Jung himself would not have assented.

Nearly as numerous as the critics are Jung's theological supporters. Among them is Hans Schaer, a Swiss Protestant theologian who occasionally lectured at the Jung Institute in the late 1940s. Far from criticizing Jung for overstepping epistemological boundaries, Schaer felt that Jung's psychology of religion (his psychological explanation of religion, especially of Christianity) rescued the latter from stagnancy and illuminated the whole religious process. For Schaer, Jung's concept of individuation explained the tenor of religious life. Surprisingly, Schaer believed that Jung's psychology was completely compatible with Christianity. When we examine Jung's concept of God we will see more clearly why this opinion was "surprising." Schaer failed to notice that Jung's psychology may—as Buber, and I, would argue—end by being a competitor of traditional religion rather than a mere illuminator of it.

Naomi Goldenberg adds her voice to those charging that Jung's psychology is religion. Or, as Goldenberg puts it, Jung "set out to construct a psychology that would function like a religion,"[8] which is perhaps not quite the same thing. Peter Homans argues that Jung's psychology "is a genuine alternative to classic Christianity, evolving, however, out of the matrix of experience that long ago produced the original doctrines."[9] Homans focuses on Jung's advocacy of the withdrawal of projections in order to activate new psychological forces, which in their turn can be made conscious and integrated. "In this sense—but in this sense only—Jung ascribed to his own system of ideas a significance functionally equivalent to traditional belief systems."[10]

My plan in this chapter is to show not only that Jung's psychology functions like a religion, but that in some senses of the word, it actually is a religion. While neither claim would be likely to please Jung, evidence can be drawn from his own statements to support them both. We will start with Jung's definition of religion, his understanding of God, and his "God-talk." Then we will look more in depth at the archetypal image of the self and its religious nature, and at Jung's concept of the archetype per se.

Noting the religiousness of Jung's psychology is essential in understanding the deeply entrenched nature of some of the Jungian concepts. The fact that androcentrism seems to be the "way things are," as I discussed in chapter 2, is not the only explanation for analytical psychology's resistance to change. If Jung's psychology is a religion, it stands as a symbol system itself, "revealed" to its founder—discovered, not invented. As a result, it rests on sacred and unassailable ground. Many psychologies give meaning, direction, and order to life, but its link to the sacred singles out analytical psychology. Being thus linked, it meets the needs of its adherents in much the same way a religion does. Events, images, and feelings take their place in a cosmic order when explained on the basis of its principles. On the level of theory, as the primary images in Jungian psychology replace traditional religious images, they partake of a sacred quality. On the level of practice, an analysand will probably experience them as numinous and transformative. Like most psychologies, Jungian psychology does not proclaim the Truth, although following it does allow one to find one's own truth. Yet Jung's psychology comes closer than many psychologies—particularly those adhering to more positivistic boundaries—to being a "way" or a "path" to truth, a further explanation for the devotion of its followers. For all these reasons, Jung's psychology is resistant to change and to criticism, like religious dogma itself. This is ironic, since Jung himself was so hostile to dogma.

In the analysis that follows, I am not claiming that Jung consciously intended to found a religious system. His repeated statements about his empiricism bear witness to his intense need to belong to the scientific community. Moreover, there is no reason not to believe his declared frustration at being taken for a mystic. What I will be looking at is "in the cracks," not in Jung's conscious intentions or statements of them. Looking in the "cracks" will mean examining some areas of confusion. For example, Jung's talk about God and the archetypal image of the self is often "muddy" and "confused," although not for that reason lacking in meaning for Jungians. The same "muddiness" is characteristic of his concept of the archetype, at least until 1946, when he distinguished it from the image. In the most generous interpretation—one favored by Jung and Jungians— these explanations are "paradoxical." I suggest, however, that some of Jung's "God-talk" is internally contradictory because it represents the "core of the complex" for Jung himself. These religious areas are those in which Jung's own search and need were the most intense, the most determined by experience, and hence the least clear. This lack of clarity was projected into analytical psychology.

Scholars of various disciplines have given widely varying definitions of religion. Anthropologists, sociologists, and psychologists, as well as theologians and philosophers, all attempt to pin religion down with definitions that reveal their own standpoint. Jung enters the definitional arena unabashedly as a psychologist, looking at religion through psychological eyeglasses. Curiously and, I think, unintentionally, the definitions of religion he offers establish analytical psychology itself as religion. In support of this, we can turn again to Jung's letter to Freud written February 11, 1910, quoted in chapter 3: "Religion can only be replaced by religion. . . . 2000 years of Christianity can only be replaced by something equivalent." Jung was very impressed with Rudolf Otto's effort to restore the nonrational dimension to religion and noted the centrality of the nonrational, or the *numinosum* (Otto's word, meaning the sacred, the holy), in analytic work. Otto argues that when faced with the numinous, humans feel the elements of "awfulness, overpoweringness, energy and urgency." On this theme Jung says:

> Religion appears to me to be a peculiar attitude of mind which could be formulated in accordance with the original use of the word *religio*, which means a *careful consideration and observation of certain dynamic factors that are conceived as "powers, spirits, daemons, gods, laws, ideas, ideals,* or whatever name man has given to such factors in his world as he has found powerful, dangerous, or helpful enough to be taken into careful consideration, or grand, beautiful and meaningful enough to be devoutly worshiped and loved. [11]

Further in the same work, Jung gives a more common definition: "One could define religious experience as that kind of
experience which is accorded the highest value, no matter what
its contents may be." [12] According to the second definition,
whether it is the Buddha, the Christ, the love of money, an
obsession with people of the opposite sex, or analytical psychology, if it is accorded the highest value, it is religion. What Jung
conveys in the first definition is more interesting and unusual,
and it applies specifically to the attitude required of an analysand in Jungian analysis. He emphasizes the quality of attention
paid to whatever seizes or compels one. His use of the word
religio implies a certain distance, an attitude of mind that can
stand back and carefully observe the powers, spirits, demons,
and gods that threaten to overwhelm. His method of dialoguing
with the unconscious encourages just this sort of distancing
during analysis. In his confrontation with the unconscious,
Jung engaged his own unconscious figures in precisely this
spirit.

In *Psychology and Religion: West and East,* the volume from
which the definitions are taken, Jung describes his work with an
atheist. Since the man was consciously an atheist, the missing
religious function was in his unconscious: "Fortunately, the man
had *religio,* that is, he 'carefully took account of' his experience.
. . . He had to confess that the unquenchable fire was 'holy.'
This was the *sine qua non* of his cure." [13]

For Jung, analytic work involves a "peculiar attitude of
mind" that carefully takes account of and observes one's experience. But does that make it religion? According to Jung's own
definition, we would have to answer in the affirmative, since
religion itself is a "quality of attention." According to Jung's
distinction between creeds and religion, his psychology is not a
creed. *Religio* and analytical psychology emphasize the importance of individual experience. Creeds, in Jung's view, would
encourage one to deny one's experience.

Besides fitting neatly into Jung's own definition of religion,
there are other characteristics of analytical psychology that
qualify it for the title "religion." The fact that even the atheist's
healing was, in the end, "religious" illustrates Jung's position
that all psychological healing is really spiritual. In an essay well
known to pastoral psychologists, "Psychotherapists or the

Clergy," he claims that "healing may be called a religious problem." [14] In an oft-quoted passage, Jung says:

> Among all my patients in the second half of life—that is to say
> over thirty-five—there has not been one whose problem in the
> last resort was not that of finding a religious outlook on life.
> . . . It is as though, at the climax of the illness, the destructive
> powers were converted into healing forces. This is brought
> about by the archetype's awakening to independent life and
> taking over the guidance of the psychic personality, thus sup-
> planting the ego with its futile willing and striving. As a
> religious-minded person would say: guidance has come from
> God. [15]

Religion is often considered transformative. Frederick Streng, for example, calls religion a "means of ultimate transformation." [16] The analytical process in which two points of view, conscious and unconscious, come into dialogue is likewise transformative.

Another window into Jung's view of religion is his theory about the breakdown of institutional religion. Jung believed that when institutional religion fails to meet human need, new religious images, symbols, and myths emerge from the collective unconscious to take their place. This fact—that new religious imagery is continually arising out of the unconscious— Jung attributed to what he called the "religious function." Without this function humans cannot survive, for humans cannot live without meaning. Analytical psychology has a special appeal for people who are dissatisfied with their religious tradition, who find it stale, lacking in inspiration, or unable to respond appropriately to the contemporary social situation. If such people are true to the Jungian way of "careful attention to the *numinosum*," they will encourage psychoreligious images to arise in their lives in dreams, fantasies, or active imagination. These orient, expand, and enrich the personality. Here Jung's psychology of religion functions both as an explanatory system and as a religion itself, since analytical psychology is one of the replacements for institutional religion that Jung is talking about.

Analytical psychology is not only a quality of attention, as I have discussed. It is also a symbol system. Although its symbols are not fixed or static theoretically, once they have been named and conceptualized, they tend to function as givens. The shadow, animus, anima, and self take on the functions previously ascribed to Jesus, the Virgin Mary, God, and the devil, becoming psychologized, "inner" versions of a religious symbol system. During the individuation process, one becomes acquainted with these images, which function as psychic, symbolic entities, or as personalities separate and distinct from the ego. That is to say, these images are like gods, and they are autonomous until integrated. Coming to know the "little people" in the psyche is not so different from coming to know Jesus or Mary or God, except that the "little people" are conceived of as psychological—that is, in the psyche—rather than as "other." Jung actually begs the question about the "outer reality" of these images since the psyche is all he can know; yet he tends to locate the figures as "inner," rather than "outer." The final, governing image, the self, is the God-image in the psyche, as we have seen. During individuation, it is understood as manifesting itself. The process of coming to know it is no different than coming to know God in traditional Christianity or Judaism, except in the person's conception of it. In analytical psychology, Jung conceived of it as part of the psyche, therefore as "psychic."

Most founders of traditional religions claim that they received a revelation of Truth. Jung's receptivity in the confrontation with his unconscious is similar to this attitude. At one point during his self-analysis, Jung came to what he called a "standstill." Although his dreams and fantasies were pregnant with imagery, he could not understand them. It seemed that "something dead was present, but it was also still alive." Unable to find any approach to his material that would work, he finally said to himself, "Since I know nothing at all, I shall simply do whatever occurs to me. Thus I consciously submitted myself to the impulses of the unconscious." [17] This description gives a religious underpinning to Jung's discoveries. Analytical psychology takes on a kind of sacred aura—a "revealed" quality—in this way. By assuming this submissive attitude toward the unconscious, Jung was practicing religion. As he said himself: "Religion is submission to and dependence upon the irrational facts of experience." [18] That Jung took this stance before the unconscious showed that for him, the unconscious was the source of religious experience.

The question remains as to the source of the revelation. Jung is clear that he submitted to the unconscious, not that he submitted to God. Yet he came very close to equating the two. Notice that Jung often uses the word "unconscious" to stand for experiences that religious people would account for with the word "God." [19] He knows this and talks about it. One of many of such disclosures appears in *Memories*. Jung describes returning home on a train and trying to read a book, but being unable to because of an overwhelming image and memory of someone drowning. Upon his return, he finds that his youngest grandchild has nearly drowned in the boathouse. "This had taken place at exactly the time I had been assailed by that memory in the train. The unconscious had given me a hint." [20] More explicit is the following account of the clash of opposites in a personality:

> Recognizing that they do not spring from his conscious personality, [the patient] calls them mana, daimon, or God. Science employs the term "the unconscious," thus admitting that it knows nothing about it. . . . Hence I prefer the term "the unconscious," knowing that I might equally well speak of "God" or "daimon" if I wished to express myself in mythic language. When I do use such mythic language, I am aware that "mana," "daimon" and "God" are synonyms for the unconscious. [21]

Here Jung distinguished between God and the unconscious by the level of discourse. Scientists using empirical discourse, Jung tells us, employ the term "the unconscious" in order to leave the matter open, whereas religious believers employ mythic language for the same phenomena. The distinction in Jung's autobiography is remarkable for its precision.

Next we will enter muddy theoretical territory, and as I suggested above, I believe this is because it is the area of Jung's own complex. Jung would probably not disagree with this assessment. For example, he let it be widely known that he wrote *Answer to Job* in what he called a "white heat," almost as a compulsion. Similarly, he wrote Abraxes' *Ten Sermons to the Dead* in a "heat," and designated this work as an exorcism of what he felt to be a "haunting." It seems fair to say that he was driven to come to terms with his God all his life. Doing so was not something over which he even claimed rational control; rather, it was a question of *religio*—a scrupulous attention to the "non-rational factors" that gripped him. One of the fuzziest areas of Jung's religious and psychological writings is his "God-talk"— that is, how he chooses to express what he considers to be God. Generally, Jung expects his readers to understand that when he says "God" he means the archetypal image of God. However, he uses the term "God" just as other people do, so naturally, readers assume he is talking about God per se and not just the image. His unclear use of terms causes perpetual confusion, especially evident in his dealings with theologians. In response to theological critiques, Jung often took refuge in his quasi-Kantian stance, saying that he was making psychological statements only—that is, having to do only with the image of God:

> Take, for instance, the word "God." The theologian will naturally assume that the metaphysical *Ens Absolutum* is meant. The empiricist, on the contrary, does not dream of making such a far-reaching assumption, which strikes him as downright impossible anyway. He just as naturally means the word "God" as a mere statement, or at most as an archetypal motif which prefigures such statements.[22]

This passage qualifies him as a "methodological agnostic." In his assertion that he is not a metaphysician or a theologian, and that in all of his statements about "God" he is speaking as a psychologist only, he claims neutrality with regard to God. As a psychologist he believes that he is merely documenting what he observes at work in the human psyche over and over again: an image of God.

Near the end of his life the British Broadcasting Company (B.B.C.) made a film about Jung. The interviewer asked him if he believed in God. Slowly, thoughtfully, turning his pipe in his hand and with an expression on his face that suggested he thought this an extraordinary question, Jung answered, "I don't need to believe. I know." How does his methodological agnosticism square with this view? Rather than jumping to the easy conclusion that one statement represents his stance as a scientist and the other his personal feeling, I suggest there is more consistency here than first meets the eye. If we take Jung at his word and accept that every time he says "God" he means an archetypal image in the psyche, we will have understood him.

Viewers of the film often respond on a deep emotional level to Jung's answer, as though he had confirmed the existence of the Divine. This is a metaphysical jump that he does not intend, even though his language leads one to it. In a letter to a critic, Jung unpacked his statement that he doesn't need to believe because he knows God exists, explaining that belief implies doubt and he has no doubt of God because he has experienced God: "I do know that I am obviously confronted with a factor unknown in itself, which I call 'God.' . . . It is an apt name given to all overpowering emotions in my own psychic system subduing my conscious will and usurping control over myself." [23] By his answer to the interviewer, we must assume Jung meant, "I know of the archetypal image of God because I have experienced its numinosity." Experience, for Jung, is knowledge. Because of his recourse to experiential knowledge as well as his obscure "God-talk," Jung is sometimes classified as a mystic. Because of it, also, he can accurately refer to himself as an "empiricist," in the second common understanding of the word: experiential. In a 1954 letter to a friend where he is clearly speaking of experience, Jung wrote: "That is *one side* of my experiences with what is called 'God.' 'Coarse' is too weak a word for it. 'Crude,' 'violent,' 'cruel,' 'bloody,' 'hellish,' 'demonic' would be better. That I was not downright blasphemous I owe to my domestication and polite cowardice." [24]

What is this "God" Jung knows? "Coarse, crude, violent, cruel, bloody, hellish, demonic" hardly describe the traditional Christian concept of God. Jung's "God" is true to his theory of the archetypal images, each one consisting of a negative and a positive pole, the tension of opposites, without which the life of the psyche could not go on. His early experience of God as both containing and being beyond opposites (for example, in the cathedral fantasy) had led him to criticize the Christian concept of God as all-good, including the old doctrine of evil as *privatio boni*. Jung's God has a "dark," "shadow," or "evil" side just as humans do. "God," as an archetypal image in the psyche, is a *coniunctio oppositorum,* a conjunction, or a complex, of opposites. In *Answer to Job* Jung says, "The conflict in [God's] nature is so great that the incarnation can only be bought by an expiatory self-sacrifice offered up to the wrath of God's dark side."[25] Jung had, in other writings, equated unconsciousness with evil, and in *Answer to Job* he applies that same understanding to God:

> The naive assumption that the creator of the world is a conscious being must be regarded as a disastrous prejudice which later gave rise to the most incredible dislocations of logic. For example, the nonsensical doctrine of the *privatio boni* would never have been necessary had one not had to assume in advance that it is impossible for the consciousness of a good God to produce evil deeds. Divine unconsciousness and lack of reflection, on the other hand, enable us to form a conception of God which puts his actions beyond moral judgment and allows no conflict to arise between goodness and beastliness.[26]

Further in the same work:

> To believe that God is the *Summum Bonum* is impossible for a reflecting consciousness. . . . It is quite right, therefore, that fear of God should be considered the beginning of all wisdom. On the other hand, the much-vaunted goodness, love, and justice of God should not be regarded as mere propitiation, but should be recognized as a genuine experience, for God is a *coincidentia oppositorum*. Both are justified, the fear of God as well as the love of God.[27]

With his archetypal image of God/self, Jung tries to rectify what he sees as an imbalance and an incompleteness in traditional Christian symbolism. His justification for the two sides of God is psychological, for he has observed that exclusion of any element relegates it to the unconscious where it can then erupt without warning. Since this law of the psyche holds true for God as well as for any other factor, it became a psychological necessity for Jung to hold that evil belongs to God as much as good does. Jung believed that God's "shadow side" can "act out," causing wanton destruction, just as a human shadow side can. He believed that exonerating God of all responsibility for evil, and subsequently attributing it to humans, kept people in a perpetual state of guilt. He raged against what he felt was this unfair attribution of all evil to humans by theologies that make God all-good. Because of the psychological consequences, it is as important in Jung's view that we have an all-inclusive God-image as it is that we embrace the wholeness in our human selves. In Jung's psychology, both God and humans need to come to "consciousness," that is, to move beyond the opposition between conscious and unconscious, rational and nonrational. God, too, (remember, "God" refers to an archetypal image inherent in the psyche) has potential wholeness and needs humans to come to consciousness in order to attain wholeness. Humans and God are inextricably bound up with one another, Jung felt, and as long as humans are unconscious of their "dark side," acting out unconsciously, so will God be partly unconscious. Jung's concept of God, Schaer's sanguine acceptance of it notwithstanding, is a primary reason that many Christian theologians have difficulty with his "theology."

We noted in *Memories* that Jung distinguished between scientific and religious language for the same phenomenon, which he said in scientific terms is called "the unconscious" and in religious terms, "God." In other writings Jung made both the distinction and the equation between God and the unconscious on different grounds, and the equation is a little more cautious. From a more scientific standpoint, in "A Psychological Approach to the Trinity," Jung wrote: "Submission to any metaphysical authority is, from the psychological standpoint, submission to the unconscious. There are no scientific criteria for distinguishing so-called metaphysical factors from psychic ones." [28] And again in *Answer to Job:* "It is only through the psyche that we can establish that God acts upon us, but we are unable to distinguish whether these actions emanate from God or from the unconscious. We cannot tell whether God and the unconscious are two different entities. Both are border-line concepts for transcendental contents." [29]

In these statements, Jung hints strongly at the equation of God and the unconscious, although he does not equate the two as boldly as he does in his autobiography where, as we saw, he attributes to his unconscious his knowledge of an accident that took place in his absence. In his autobiography, which he dictated to his secretary Aniela Jaffe at the end of his life, perhaps Jung felt able to be fully himself, with no more bows toward a mocking scientific community. Putting his statements together, it seems fair to say that experientially—which, for Jung, is the level of the real—God and the unconscious are one and the same. As a scientist, he says, he cannot distinguish between the two. If this is so, then archetypal images, which "emanate" from the collective unconscious, are manifestations of God in human life. They are divinely ordained. They stand on sacred ground.

James Heisig shows that Jung gradually divinized his concept of the collective unconscious: "Jung showed no hesitation in referring to the cornerstone of his psychology—the collective unconscious—as God, convinced as he was that he was speaking of the very thing that men at all times and places have called God."[30] After detailing Jung's trajectory of religious thought, Heisig concludes: "Each of these adaptations of the theory of the collective unconscious encouraged his gradual reification of the collective unconscious. From a quasi-substance it became a cosmic principle."[31] Jung's gradual equation of God and the unconscious adds substance to the argument that analytical psychology is a religion, since the practice of analytical psychology allows people to come to terms with the unconscious. Using Jung's own suggestive language, we would have to conclude that Jungian analysis is a pathway to God.

What I have just laid out may be confusing because, although it provides an accurate depiction of his near equation of God and the unconscious, Jung is himself inconsistent. At times he clearly designates a specific image in the unconscious to stand for God. This is the image of the self, the emergence of which is central to the individuation process. In a more precise explanation of the relationship between the unconscious and God, Jung states: "Strictly speaking, the God-image does not coincide with the unconscious as such, but with a special content of it, namely the archetype of the self. It is this archetype from which we can no longer distinguish the God-image empirically."[32] We can infer that readers must have frequently misunderstood Jung's equation of the God-image and the self-image, for we find him insistently defending his equation of the archetypal image of the self with God against the claim that he has replaced God with the self. In a letter to a critic, Jung said: "It is a misunderstanding to accuse me of having made out of this an 'immanent God' or a 'God-substitute.' . . . This 'self' never at any time takes the place of God, though it may perhaps be a vessel for divine grace."[33] His defense rests once again on his quasi-Kantian epistemology: "You seem not to have noticed that I speak of the

God-image and *not of God* because it is quite beyond me to say anything about God at all."[34] Jung equates the image of God with the image of the self because of a profound transformation he observed: this transformation was taking place in his own imagery, in that of his patients, and finally, in the collective at large. Traditional God-images, Jung noted, were being replaced by images of the self, or wholeness. When Jung, then, replaced the term "God" with self (both are archetypal images), he understood himself to be on firm phenomenological ground, reporting what he observed. Regarding the self he says: "It stands for the goal of the total man, for the realization of his wholeness and individuality with or without the consent of his will."[35]

For Jung, self and God symbols represent the highest values and meanings in human life. The implication is that nothing can be excluded from this modern God-image. As Heisig notes: "Jung gives himself every latitude in defining the *imago Dei* and we are hard put to come up with even one image that could not in some context qualify as an instance of it."[36] The problem with a concept that is so all-inclusive, however, is that with it Jung has drawn no critical boundaries. As we have seen, just about anything—especially if it is numinous—can qualify as an expression of God under certain circumstances.

If images of the self are replacing traditional images of God, Jung felt, this shows that "man" is gradually replacing God. In a letter to Father Victor White, he explains the meaning of the age of Aquarius, which he believed was nearly upon us. This age "is certainly a oneness, presumably that of the Anthropos, the realization of Christ's allusion: '*Dii estis.*' This is a formidable secret and difficult to understand, because it means that man will be essentially God and God man."[37]

We have noted that Jung made a distinction between the archetype and the archetypal image. Here we will explore the religious nature of the archetype in itself. We find a clue as to its nature in the kind of language Jung and Jungians use to write about it. For example, they seem to consider the archetype paradoxical, and paradox represents the height of religious expression. Jolande Jacobi writes: "For the archetype represents a profound riddle surpassing our rational comprehension: 'An archetypal content expresses itself, first and foremost, in metaphors;' there is some part of its meaning that always remains unknown and defies formulation."[38] Jung himself resorts to religious language to talk about his central concept, betraying his disregard for the empiricism to which, at other times, he clings:

> Not for a moment dare we succumb to the illusion that an archetype can be finally explained and disposed of. Even the best attempts at explanation are only more or less successful translations into another metaphorical language. (Indeed, language itself is only an image.) The most we can do is to *dream the myth onwards* and give it a modern dress.[39]

In other attempts to define the archetype, Jung relies on decidedly religious language: "On account of its transcendence, the archetype *per se* is as irrepresentable as the nature of light."[40] "I don't know whether the archetype is 'true' or not. I only know that it lives and that I have not made it."[41] Jung's inability to define his central concept gives it a feeling of "ineffability." His reluctance to impose the limits inherent in a definition reminds one of others' unwillingness to define the Divine.

Sometimes Jung rationalized his lack of conceptual clarity by declaring that the highest forms of knowledge can only be conveyed by paradox. It seems that he truly believed that his work was concerned with something beyond the limits of language:

> It does more justice to the *unknowable* than clarity can do, for uniformity of meaning robs the mystery of its darkness and sets it up as something that is *known*. That is a usurpation, and it leads the human intellect into hybris by pretending that it, the intellect, has got hold of the transcendental mystery by a cognitive act and has "grasped it."[42]

Jung attributes to the archetype a kind of omniscience. This, too, suggests divinity: "Over the whole procedure there seems to reign a dim foreknowledge not only of the pattern but of its meaning."[43] He also suggests that the archetype has a "karma aspect," by which he seems to mean that that which is intended to be, will be: "The *karma* aspect is essential to a deeper understanding of the nature of an archetype."[44]

The archetypal images are, in the final analysis, forces with which humans have to reckon: "It is indeed hard to see how one can escape the sovereign power of the primordial images. Actually, I do not believe it can be escaped. *One can only alter one's attitude* and thus save oneself from naively falling into an archetype and being forced to act a part at the expense of one's humanity."[45] Jung's choice of words imputes Godlike, "inescapable" power to the archetype and its images. The most we can hope for is increased self-knowledge, self-awareness, so that we are not in opposition to ourselves and in a state of "unconsciousness."

It seems fair to say that Jung saw his theories as dealing with the center and mystery of the nature of being. Although he does not use expressly metaphysical terms or make metaphysical claims, he does use religious, mythic, and metaphorical language. He tries to avoid the metaphysical level by sticking strictly to the observation of experience and images, yet his language points beyond it. By his use of paradox and his justification of it, he conveys the impression that analytical psychology is concerned with something much grander, deeper, and more awesome than Freud allowed himself with psychoanalysis. Again Jung's letter of 1912 comes to mind, in which he asked Freud to consider whether there was a revivifying myth in psychoanalysis. Freud replied in the negative, leaving to Jung the task of "replacing religion with religion." Especially with regard to his central concept, the archetype, Jung appears to believe that he is talking about something much larger than ordinary human discourse can embrace. Like any theologian, Jung finds himself grasping for language beyond the limits of empiricism and logical analysis—an ironic position for him, in view of his oft-repeated defenses of his pure empiricism.

The "sovereign" power Jung attributes to the images invites feminist attention. As "sovereign," the images would seem an unchangeable part of the divinely ordained order of things, frustratingly unchallengeable. Jung's language suggests that all the images, including the "feminine" and the "masculine," have the quality of immutability locked in the theory, whether we choose to see them as social constructions or not. At other times, however, Jung seemed to give the images more flexibility—in his distinction between the archetype per se and its images, for example. I think the truest reading here is one that remains on the level of experience; Jung is saying that the images *feel* "sovereign," not that they are unchangeable. The archetype itself is unchangeable, and that is what gives the images such power. In any case, Jung believed that, unknown and unbefriended, the collective unconscious is so powerful that reason and will are nothing against it:

> As a matter of fact, we are constantly living on the edge of a volcano, and there is, so far as we know, no way of protecting ourselves from a possible outburst that will destroy everybody within reach. It is certainly a good thing to preach reason and common sense, but what if you have a lunatic asylum for an audience or a crowd in a collective frenzy? There is not much difference between them because the madman and the mob are both moved by impersonal, overwhelming forces.[46]

Jung's archetype-as-such is the "sacred canopy" over the whole system of images, lending it ontological and religious overtones. This gives the personifications (shadow, anima, animus, self) the status of truly religious symbols that can merely hint at an unnameable Reality. They are its various manifestations. We have now crossed the border between psychology and religion: here, Jung's psychology becomes religion itself—even though Jung still sees himself as giving psychological explanations for religion.

As a religion, analytical psychology is not exclusivist. One can follow it and be at the same time a Christian, Buddhist, Jew, Hindu, especially if one is not inclined to quibble over Jung's concept of God. Moreover, if one is both a follower of a traditional religion and a Jungian, the archetypal perspective is likely to illumine one's understanding of one's religion and its symbols, translating its terms into archetypal images. Jung's central concept, the archetype, undermines the uniqueness of any religion. If the archetype is thought to be the level of the Real, this challenges the supremacy of any particular characterization of the Divine and relegates that supremacy to the archetype. As Homans says, "Though the good Catholic or Protestant may not know it, his religious faith is motivated by the forces analytical psychology describes. The conceptualization of these forces constitutes a system of ideas and a corresponding reality very different from traditional faith."[47] With the archetype as the governing concept, analytical psychology is a religion that transcends and embraces the religions of the world. Central to its core process, individuation, is the joining of opposites, especially the opposition of the "feminine" and the "masculine."

Analytical psychology's core symbols do not demand worship. In fact, worship per se is not part of the process, unless careful attention to the *numinosum* is seen as worship. Jungian analysis demands a "worshipful" attitude, but since the numinous images are considered part of one's own psyche and experience, there is no worship in the sense of adoring an exalted being outside of oneself. As Buber claimed, Jung's religion is one of psychic immanence. This is, in fact, one of the reasons some feminist theologians appreciate him. Using this aspect of his thought, they foresee an important shift in theology, for as Naomi Goldenberg says, "feminist theology is on its way to becoming psychology." [48]

"Trust your own experience" is one of the hallmarks of Jung's religion. Peter Homans explains how this fits into the context of our day. Jung founded his psychoreligion on the authority of experience, which in his case and that of his patients was numinous and transformative. Following Jung's psychological method has opened up dimensions of spirituality in many peoples' lives where the living stream had gone dry. Inasmuch as analytical psychology is corroborated by the experience of patients in analysis, it is as irrefutable as religious experience is, and shares the same quality: it is transformative and meaning-giving.

There is no central historical figure in this religion, unless it is Jung himself. Jung's remarkable openness about his successful confrontation with his inner figures and his unusual ability to hold the opposites in tension appeals to those who are looking for a path through their own confusion and seeking to understand the collective confusion of our time. Jung appears to have found a way through his own pain and even to have come out on the other side with some wisdom. The fact that he successfully negotiated his way through his own "dark waters" may account, in part, for his great popularity and charisma. He provides a model and encouragement for other seekers. Even though he makes no claims to being a saviour, he seems to have functioned as a guru among his followers. Jung believed that people usually misunderstood the Christian doctrine of the *imitatio Dei,* trying to imitate the Christ, when Christ really called them to become fully themselves. To imitate Jung, then, would be to fall into the same folly. Theoretically, as the self manifests itself increasingly in a human life, the individual becomes uniquely herself or himself—not an imitation of any other.

There are dangers in this as there are in any religion or worldview. I have mentioned some already, including the lack of external referent. This lack makes criticism difficult, since in Jung's view, every statement one can make about the psyche comes from within the psyche. One can never take a standpoint outside of the psyche to comment upon it. Therefore any criticism one might make of analytical psychology could be taken as evidence of an unworked-through complex or insufficient knowledge of the archetypal images.

This does not mean that Jung's psychology bears no resemblance to science, or that it is hopelessly mystical and obscure as critics have charged. On the contrary, Jung did not ever depart from empiricism in its broadest sense (being based on experience), and he was true to it in its more narrow sense (being based in data gathering, experiment, and observation) at the beginning of his quest. The breadth of his mind and the depth of his spiritual search, however, reveal a dimension beyond empiricism. But this still would not exclude him from the domain of science according to contemporary philosophy of science. Philosophers of science challenge the view that science is locked into pure positivism or that the notions of empiricism fully account for what scientists do. They challenge science's claim of "objectivity," pointing out that choice of data and perception of it are influenced by the viewpoint of the observer. The "viewpoint" would include the observer's cultural, racial, and gender bias. These philosophers have further observed that scientists form mental models that go beyond material evidence, and that although they expect to let go of them once they are disproven, scientists do become attached to their models and letting go of them often proves difficult. The models then function as worldviews, helping in the selection of new data. Like most scientists, Jung became attached to his model at some point in his development, although he spoke of his willingness to give it up if a better one came along. A scientist's (or a religious believer's) commitment to a model forms a barrier against new insight, or against the well-known "paradigm shift" that Thomas Kuhn brought to public attention. Because analytical psychology is scientific, as well as religious, the resistance to a paradigm shift can operate on both levels.[49]

Women's challenge to the claims of universality of analytical psychology fall along the lines suggested by the philosophy of science. Women are claiming that in some ways they stand outside of the psyche that Jung proclaimed as universal. Rooted in their experience as women, particularly their "consciousness-raised experience," by which they have learned to detect sexism and the internalized oppression it fosters, they can challenge certain dimensions of Jung's view of the unconscious—dimensions stemming from his androcentrism. As I have shown, if the images, including animus and anima, are manifestations of the Divine, they take on extrahuman legitimation. Although it may not be explicitly recognized by Jungians today, this hint of the Divine makes it difficult to see the images in a different light from within Jungian theory itself.

More self-consciously than most scientists of his day, Jung brought himself to his experiment. He was remarkably aware that the personhood of the scientist influences the choice and perception of data. He seems, in fact, to have been himself more conscious of the problem of possible lack of objectivity in the theories than his followers have been. He spoke, for example, about men's inability to understand women's psychology because of their anima projections: "Most of what men say about feminine eroticism, and particularly about the emotional life of women, is derived from their own anima projections and distorted accordingly."[50] Therefore, in spite of analytical psychology's impressive religious overtones and the sacred legitimation of the images that this entails, it should be possible even from within Jungian theory to challenge androcentrism.

6

ANALYTICAL PSYCHOLOGY THROUGH A FEMINIST LENS

Androcentrism and misogyny distort Jung's discussions of women, the anima and animus, and the feminine. As a result, Jung's individuation process itself may be skewed for women. The infiltration of Jung's cultural and gender bias is deep enough that analytical psychology, as a body of theory, does not contain an adequate definition of women and the feminine on terms that substantiate women's "consciousness-raised" experience. Women readers and analysands need to recognize and challenge these elements of Jung's psychology or it will remain a seductive trap, luring them with compelling images of the "feminine," and thereby contributing to our lack of awareness of the internalized oppression that can be fostered by use of his categories. Interestingly, among Jungian analysts, it is a man who has most clearly challenged Jung's androcentrism at the level of theory. I refer to James Hillman, who in his most recent work, *Anima,* forthrightly recognizes the limits of Jung's position. Edward Whitmont, also a Jungian analyst, has attempted some revisions of Jung's anima/animus theory. Some female Jungian analysts (for example, Irene de Castillejo) also have challenged the one-sidedness of Jung's ascription of anima to males only, and the predominantly negative character of the animus, but Hillman has gone the furthest toward systematically revising Jung's categories.[1] Jungian scholars—non-analysts—have likewise taken significant steps toward re-visioning Jung's theories. A prominent example is the work of Estella Lauter and Carol Schreier Rupprecht, as I discussed in chapter 1.[2] By examining aspects of the theory with an awareness of the patriarchal context that it reflects, we can observe the effects of the context on the archetypal images. Thus grounded in their social context, the images can be freed from their ontological overtones and religiously legitimating potential.

As I declared earlier, "sexism and its psychological companion in women, internalized oppression, are still so widespread in our society that any psychological theory and practice that does not take those facts into account and oppose them unrelentingly is not a freeing therapy for women." Divesting Jungian psychology of its potential for reinforcing internalized oppression in women will therefore be our task.

WOMEN AND THE ANNIHILATION OF THE EGO

We saw in chapter 4 that Jung's vision of individuation starts with an assumption of an ego that believes itself to be "master in its house"—an assumption that Jung shows to be ultimately illusory. My claim here is that Jung's understanding of ego is more appropriately applied to men than to women, many of whom do not feel their ego's mastery in the first place. During individuation, theoretically, the ego comes to realize that its feeling of supremacy is false, as its "centrality" is replaced by an increasing governance of the archetype of the self. This discovery process requires the transcendence of the limits of the personal ego, and in this it resembles the traditional religions. Feminist theologians have demonstrated that such religions start, unconsciously, from the male point of view. Their recommendations of ego-transcendence therefore reflect a fitting task for males. Traditionally in patriarchy, males seem to have a stronger sense of self (firmer ego boundaries) than do females, and male agency and authority are constantly validated. Let me be clear: I believe that everyone needs a perspective beyond the necessarily limited one of the personal ego or self. Yet I wonder about urging this vision of self-development on people who are not strongly based in the ego in the first place.[3] Such is the condition of most women in patriarchy, whose egos are not validated by their context. Here I am using the term "ego" to include "sense of self," "identity," "personal agency," as well as "center of consciousness." The last meaning is the preferred Jungian one; "personal agency" the least likely Jungian meaning. Patriarchal women are tacitly and explicitly discouraged from gratifying their own needs or seeking fulfillment of their own desires. In the face of such deprivation—furthered by psychologies and theologies that have defined women's fulfillment in terms of their service to others—many women in patriarchy lack a sense of themselves as persons, or agents, in their own right.

Feminist theories, in fact, differentiate between the ego in men and in women. Jung does not. Jean Baker Miller goes so far as to suggest that ego, as it is traditionally understood, may not even exist in women:

> Prevailing psychoanalytic theories about women's weaker ego or super-ego may well reflect the fact that women have no ego or super-ego at all as these terms are used now. Women do not come into this picture in the way men do. They do not have the right or the requirement to be full-fledged representatives of the culture. Nor have they been granted the right to act and to judge themselves in terms of the direct benefit to themselves. Both of these rights seem essential to the development of ego and super-ego. This does not mean that women do not have organizing principles or relate to a "reality" in a particular way. But women's reality *is* rooted in the encouragement to "form" themselves into the person who will be of benefit to others. They thus see their own actions only as these actions are mediated through others. This experience begins at birth and continues through life. Out of it, women develop a psychic structuring for which the term ego, as ordinarily used, may not apply.[4]

If Miller's observation is true, it casts some doubt on the advisability, for women, of undergoing a crucial stage in the Jungian individuation process—"annihilation of the ego." This stage, according to Jung, prepares the way for the birth of the self (the God-image). Men whose need for control and domination is reinforced by patriarchy, who have experienced the ego's "mastery," probably do need to recognize the illusory, dangerous, as well as finally disappointing, nature of ego control—

either of oneself or of others. "Annihilation of the ego" may open the way to that recognition. For many women, however, Jung advocates by this process their "annihilating" something they may not even have. Or if they have it, it may be so wounded as to need building-up, not "annihilation." While Jung by no means intended to encourage feminine pathology, in fact was not even aware of that possibility in his individuation process, his term "annihilation" comes close to reinforcing the self-abnegation in which women already engage, to their detriment. It is not a "healthy" self-abnegation; it is closer to socially prescribed masochism.

Nancy Chodorow has also written about the way in which women's egos differ from men's. She suggests that "there is a tendency in women toward boundary confusion and a lack of sense of separateness from the world." However, she also points out that "most women do develop ego boundaries and a sense of separate self."[5] If indeed "boundary confusion" is an issue for most women, "boundary strengthening" is needed. This might take place through reinforcement of the ego (a woman's sense of self) as viable and separate from others, and through a heightening of a woman's right to personal agency and empowerment. Words like "submission" and "annihilation of the ego" reinforce a tendency already present in most patriarchal women. I have already mentioned their appropriateness for most patriarchal males.

Jung seems to share Chodorow's insight regarding women's tendency toward "boundary confusion," since he calls women's consciousness "diffuse" and men's "focused." ("Consciousness" is a bigger term for Jung than "ego," and as far as I can find, he never defines it. He means, I gather, "a conscious way of being in and perceiving the world.") What is strange is that he did not factor the difference between men's and women's consciousness into the individuation process. He posited the latter in universal terms. Women's "diffuse" consciousness, he felt, was closer to the principle of Eros (relatedness), and men's "focused" one to the principle of Logos (analysis). Jung, however, sees Eros and Logos as natural—even as archetypal principles—rather than as culturally created tendencies in women and men. That makes a crucial difference between his and most feminists' views.

From the theological vantage point, Carol Christ has written poignantly about the depth of "egolessness" in women in patriarchy: "The spiritual quest of a modern woman begins in the experience of nothingness, the experience of being without an adequate image of self."[6] Remember Polly Young-Eisendrath's statement that all adult women in this society evaluate themselves as uniquely deficient or inadequate. Women listening to the voice of internalized oppression, personified as the self-hater, need a conviction of their right to exist. Following Jung's process of coming to know the "little people" in the psyche, and ultimately the self, might give women this conviction. However, Jung in advocating the "annihilation of the ego" assumes erroneously that the state of the ego is the same in men and in women. He fails to account in his model for the constant toll that misogynist society takes on women's egos, and thus he perpetuates an illusion of equality between men and women. Women are greatly helped by seeing that their demolished egos are the price of living in a society that devalues them: they benefit from realizing that their wounded state is not solely a private problem.

I said earlier that women, like men, need a perspective beyond the limited one of the personal ego. Women, too, need to "die" to something before a new self can be born. But is it the ego we need to "die to"? A possible re-visioning of Jung's process can be posed in relational terms. For example, perhaps men need to undergo the annihilation of an ego experienced as separate and distinct from others and to be reborn into relationality. This is suggested already by the images of *coniunctio* (male and female, conjoined) that Jung uses to symbolize the birth of the new self. Perhaps women, on the other hand, need to die to the false self system that patriarchy has imposed on them, whatever form it has taken. This is not the same thing as the annihilation of the ego, but dying to the false self would necessarily precede the birth of the true self. The result of this "death" could be, as with men, a capacity for true relationality.[7]

THE PRIMAL POWER OF IMAGES: ANIMA

Elizabeth Dodson Gray, a feminist theologian, has characterized the nature of patriarchy as conceptual: "Patriarchy has erroneously conceptualized and mythed 'Man's place' in the universe and thus—by the illusion of dominion that it legitimates—it endangers the entire planet."[8] Feeding the erroneous concepts and myths Dodson Gray speaks of are unworked-through, unconscious images accompanied by primal emotions. In other words, even more powerful than concepts are images, because they are more primary. Recall the enormous power Jung attributes to images as we begin our examination of the anima. It is a "concept," but it is also an image.

Jung mentioned men's inability to perceive women clearly because of their anima projections, yet his own discussions of anima confusingly intermingle anima and the psychology of women. As a result, out of Jung's depictions of the anima emerge two blurred agendas. He often states specifically that he is going to discuss the anima—an aspect of male psychology—and then launches into a discussion of the psychology of women. Jung's declared agenda, then, is to discuss this "contrasexual other" (anima) in the lives and psyches of men, but the unintentional agenda covers the psychology of women. The two discussions are logically connected, of course, since men's anima projections and women's psychology cannot help but be interrelated. Since we all tend to become who we are addressed as being, men's anima projections help shape women's sense of self.[9] But Jung does not follow these two agendas in logical sequence. Instead, he projects his own anima willy-nilly into the discussions of women's psychology. Had he separated his own anima projections from his accounts of women's psychology, the latter, especially, would be clearer. Had he located both discussions within the context of patriarchy's influence on men's anima images and women's sense of self, both would be improved. In *Two Essays,* for example, Jung begins his treatment of the anima by talking about how women other than a man's mother may influence the "feminine" aspect of his personality:

> In the place of the parents, woman now takes up her position as the most immediate environmental influence in the life of the adult man. . . . She is, however, a very influential factor and, like the parents, she produces an imago of a relatively autonomous nature—not an imago to be split off like that of the parents, but one that has to be kept associated with consciousness.

In the next passage, however, remarks about the psychology of women intrude into Jung's treatment of anima:

> Woman, with her very dissimilar psychology, is and always has been a source of information about things for which a man has no eyes. She can be his inspiration; her intuitive capacity, often superior to man's, can give him timely warning, and her feeling, always directed towards the personal, can show him ways which his own less personally accented feeling would never have discovered.[10]

This unacknowledged intrusion of women's psychology into the discussion of anima works like subliminal advertising to give women a hidden message about who they are: it is a message that a woman can imbibe without consciously knowing either that she has taken it in or where it came from. It says that woman's identity is found in the service of a man. Since this message is couched in flattering terms that coincide with the self-image that patriarchal women have been trained to prefer, many will not notice its androcentrism. It is a particularly seductive and dangerous message for women whom Jungians call "father's daughters." These are women who, loved and validated by their fathers and loving and trusting their fathers in turn, derive their sense of self-worth from being pleasing to men. Partly because their fathers have fostered their abilities these women—however successful in the "outer" world—still seek approval from men. The effect of Jung's theory, however unintended, is to undermine women's feeling of self-worth in themselves.

In the next section of the same essay, Jung repeats this confusing maneuver. He starts by saying that a man's own femininity is another reason for the "feminine nature of the soul-complex":

> There is no question here of any linguistic "accident," of the kind that makes the sun feminine in German and masculine in other languages. We have, in this matter, the testimony of art from all ages, and besides that the famous question: *Habet mulier animam?* [Does woman have a soul?] Most men, probably, who have any psychological insight at all will know what Rider Haggard means by "she-who-must-be-obeyed."

The next line leaps into women's psychology once again:

Moreover they know at once the kind of woman who most readily embodies this mysterious factor, of which they have so vivid a premonition.[11]

This passage injects invalidation of women into the discussion of anima ("Does woman have a soul?" "mysterious factor," and "she-who-must-be-obeyed"). Here Jung's own anima is clearly distorting his perception of women. This anima is so powerful as to upset his capacity to see real women. There is a tragic irony, moreover, in the lack of consistency between his, and most men's, perceptions of women (via their anima projections) as incredibly powerful and women's experience of their own powerlessness. This irony is not challenged in Jung's theory, nor by his followers, because of the near universality of andro-centrism. Many female Jungians have corroborated Jung's de-valuation of women because their own internalized oppression is reassuringly in tune with his opinions.

In others of his works, Jung repeats the same confusion of anima and female psychology. The following passage, like the others, is taken from a description of anima:

Finally it should be remarked that *emptiness* is a great femi-nine secret. It is something absolutely alien to man; the chasm, the unplumbed depths, the *yin*. The pitifulness of this vacuous nonentity goes to his heart (I speak here as a man), and one is tempted to say that this constitutes the whole "mystery" of women. Such a female is fate itself. A man may say what he likes about it; be for it or against it, or both at once, in the end he falls, absurdly happy, into this pit, or, if he doesn't, he has missed and bungled his only chance of making a man of himself.[12]

Describing women in these terms does nothing to restore their sense of worth, nor does it address the issue of the wounded-ness of women in patriarchy who end up "empty." Even though this passage has a romantic overtone, it is damaging to women to be seen and described as "other." As a result of the prevalence of such descriptions, women learn to experience themselves in alienated terms. Equally damaging is the use women suffering from internalized oppression can make of such a passage to learn how to capture a man, since "capturing a man" is felt to compen-sate for women's lack of recognition and worth in themselves. By association with a man who has status, recognition, and a strong sense of worth, a woman may unconsciously be trying to acquire those qualities. But such association is a far cry from coming to recognize one's worth in oneself, and it fails to address the central issue.

Jung's depictions of the anima continue to reveal characteristics that he attributes to women, for example, woman's "magic authority." [13] As in the phrase "she-who-must-be-obeyed" in the quotation above, Jung's imputation of "magic authority" to women, juxtaposed with women's actual experience, is tragic. Again, its only usefulness is in awakening us to the enormous power of the anima itself. With an anima as powerful as this, it is not surprising that men have tried to depotentiate women in the social sphere. Since they tend to confuse their animas with real women, the combination of powerful animas and powerful women would overwhelm them. Thus men need to keep real women from gaining real power, authority, and respect in the "outer" world. Such manmade theories are confusing to women, who do not experience themselves as powerful but who receive the message from men (and from theories like this one) that they are. Since such theories reflect patriarchal society's fear of women, they reinforce women's difficulty in claiming their right to authority and empowerment.

Jung's treatments of anima continue by naming "indefiniteness" and "passivity" as female traits—traits especially dominant in women who identify with their mothers:

> First, they are so empty that a man is free to impute to them anything he fancies. In addition, they are so unconscious that the unconscious puts out countless invisible feelers, veritable octopus-tentacles, that suck up all masculine projections; and this pleases men enormously. All that feminine indefiniteness is the longed-for counterpart of male decisiveness and single-mindedness, which can be satisfactorily achieved only if a man can get rid of everything doubtful, ambiguous, vague, and muddled by projecting it upon some charming example of feminine innocence. Because of the woman's characteristic passivity, and the feelings of inferiority which make her continually play the injured innocent, the man finds himself cast in an attractive role. [14]

Here Jung comes dangerously close to patronizing women, as if women are pets to be indulged but not taken seriously. Nonetheless, there is also some insight into women's psychology ("feelings of inferiority which make her continually play the injured innocent"). Without a recognition of patriarchy's role in creating this pathology, however, Jung's diagnosis lacks a dimension that is needed to heal and change. Patriarchal society values "feminine indefiniteness." Feminine definiteness, combined with the power of the anima, indeed appears to threaten.

If women who identify with their mothers are troubled by indefiniteness, Jung finds those with a "negative mother complex" even more problematic. Such a woman, Jung believes, is plagued by an exacting criticalness, a resistant temperament, a tendency to look back instead of forward into life. If she can overcome such tendencies, however, she can make an excellent partner for a man, because "as the spiritual guide and adviser of a man, such a woman, unknown to the world, may play a highly influential part":

> This woman is not frightening to a man, because she builds bridges for the masculine mind over which he can safely guide his feelings to the opposite shore. Her clarity of understanding inspires him with confidence. . . . The understanding possessed by this type of woman will be a guiding star to him in the darkness and seemingly unending mazes of life. [15]

Jung again directly promotes internalized oppression in women and demonstrates the depth of his androcentrism. Women reading it will tend to type themselves either as the woman who "is not frightening to a man" or as the implied one who is. A woman's worth, in other words, is measured by the degree to which she does not frighten men. The woman who does not pose a threat to men can make her apparent good fortune the occasion for asserting her superiority over women who do frighten men. Having been deprived of power herself, she in turn "puts down" her less "attractive" sister. In either case, the man's point of view prevails.

One positive insight emerges, however. The anima is clearly an immensely powerful force in the male psyche. If women realize that men are perceiving their animas, not women themselves, in these kinds of statements about women's psychology, they will find them less confusing. Jung's concept of the anima is useful in unraveling the confusion that reigns between the sexes, and particularly in the area of male-made psychologies of women.

Jung, by conceptualizing the anima projection, names and illuminates a pervasive phenomenon for other male psychologists. Let us look explicitly at the anima in terms of "her" effects in men's lives. Recall Jung's adoption of Rudolf Otto's term "the numinous" to describe the power of the archetypal images. Otto applied the term to the power of the Divine. The numinous, Otto says, evokes the feeling of the uncanny, the eerie, the weird, a daemonic dread, an unnatural, extraordinary fear, the feeling of awefulness, overpoweringness, the element of energy, urgency, the wholly other, and fascination. Otto clearly means these words to convey a strong mixture of fear and attraction. For Jung, the anima contains just that mix. Such an exalted ambivalence has significant implications for a man's perception of the "feminine" side of himself. Jung's pairing of the fear and attraction comes through clearly in the following passage:

> The mother has from the outset a decidedly symbolical significance for a man, which probably accounts for his strong tendency to idealize her. Idealization is a hidden apotropaism; one idealizes whenever there is a secret fear to be exorcized. What is feared is the unconscious and its magical influence.[16]

Again, Jung's androcentrism skews the model for women. Are women to assume we have a closer association with the unconscious and its "magical influence" than men have? In some ways, of course, we may—ways well explained by Jean Baker Miller, who shows that subordinates nearly always understand dominants better than the other way around. If women have such understanding, it may seem to men to represent the "unconscious" and its "magical influence," but it can be better explained by men's and women's relative positions in society. Subordinates have to understand dominants; sometimes their very survival depends on it.[17]

Jung's account of the mother's significance is conspicuously one-sided, lacking in empathy for the person who is feared. The woman/mother is made an object, an other. Empathy is similarly lacking in Jung's understanding of woman in this passage on the anima:

> Every mother and every beloved is forced to become the carrier and embodiment of this omnipresent and ageless image, which corresponds to the deepest reality in a man. It belongs to him,

this *perilous* image of Woman; she stands for the loyalty which in the interests of life he must sometimes forego; she is the much needed compensation for the risks, struggles, sacrifices that all end in disappointment; she is the solace for all the bitterness of life. And, at the same time, she is the great illusionist, the seductress, who draws him into life with her Maya—and not only into life's reasonable and useful aspects, but into its frightful paradoxes and ambivalences where good and evil, success and ruin, hope and despair counter-balance one another. Because she is his greatest danger she demands from a man his greatest, and if he has it in him, she will receive it. . . . there is every likelihood that the numinous qualities which make the mother imago so dangerously powerful derive from the collective archetype of the anima, which is incarnated anew in every male child. [18]

Edward Whitmont describes men's "secret fear" of the anima even more specifically: "Fear and attraction, in fact, always go together in the confrontation of the world of the absolutely other, the other sex. . . . Even in the case of a good relationship between mother and son the pattern of expectation in regard to women has its element of secret fear." [19] One is struck by Whitmont's choice of the words "the world of the absolutely other" to describe women. The "Absolutely Other" is a term sometimes applied to God. To apply it to women suggests, once again, that the anima projection renders men incapable of perceiving the humanness of women. Like Jung's, Whitmont's description of the anima reveals men's fear of real women and of the "feminine" within themselves. There is no problem from a feminist perspective with the realization that men fear and are attracted to women and to what they have called the "feminine." Located within the context of patriarchy, an understanding of men's fear of women, and its correspondence to the anima, might serve as a starting point for the healing of misogyny. This purpose, however, is not served by Jung and Whitmont's awe-filled, compelling, contextless images. Jung and Whitmont elevate men's fear of women to the level of symbol and mythologize it, rather than challenging the fear itself. Their efforts are then directed toward coming into conscious relationship with their animas. This attempt is a confusing half-step in the right direction, but it lacks the healing power it could have if the model accounted for patriarchy's devaluation of women and truly considered this all-absorbing male fear.

Ernest Becker's celebrated book *The Denial of Death* sheds light on the origin of this fear. In the following passage, Becker discusses every child's horror at the discovery of their vulnerability and physicalness, taking the male perspective and generalizing it as universal.

> The real threat of the mother comes to be connected with her sheer physicalness. Her genitals are used as a convenient focus for the child's obsession with the problem of physicalness. If the mother is a goddess of light, she is also a witch of the dark. He sees her tie to the earth, her secret bodily processes that bind her to nature; the breast with its mysterious sticky milk, the menstrual odors and blood, the almost continual immersion of the productive mother in her corporeality, and not least—something the child is very sensitive to—the often neurotic and helpless character of this immersion. After the child gets hints about the mother's having babies, sees them being nursed, gets a good look at the toiletful of menstrual blood that seems to leave the witch quite intact and unconcerned, there is no question about her immersion in stark body-meanings and body-fallibilities. The mother must exude determinism, and the child expresses his horror at his complete dependency on what is physically vulnerable. And so we understand not only the boy's preference for masculinity but also the girl's "penis-envy." Both boys and girls succumb to the desire to flee the sex represented by the mother; they need little coaxing to identify with the father and his world. He seems more neutral physically, more cleanly powerful, less immersed in body determinisms; he seems more "symbolically free," represents the vast world outside the home, social world with its organized triumph over nature, the very escape from contingency that the child seeks.[20]

This stark passage, read with feminist eyes, comes close to revealing the source of the fear. Like Jung and Whitmont, Becker completely lacks compassion for the mother he describes. His fear of embodiment is so great, and so completely projected on the "mother," that it alienates him from her. Since his anima projection on her is nearly total, he is prevented from appreciating how it might feel to be the object of such loathing. Although Becker is aware of a universalized fear of "physicalness," dependency, and vulnerability, he shies away from acknowledging the qualities he fears as his own. His defense against such an acknowledgment is to project those qualities on the mother and to spread general alienation—by pronouncing the fear to be universal and the qualities "feminine"—from the human experience of embodiment. His fear seems to be of the organic, decaying, earthbound, and material. The words he chooses to describe the man—"more neutral physically," "more cleanly powerful"—express his desire to dissociate himself from the material. Becker's description illustrates Western men's desire, generally, to escape the implications of embodiment. Such an escape involves projecting that essential aspect of being human onto an other—the female.

Jung made much of the etymological link between the words "mother" and "matter"; both stem from the Latin *mater*. "Mother earth" was an important metaphor for him. Let Becker's description of the "cleanly powerful" character of the man and the "continual immersion of the productive mother in her corporeality" stand behind Jung's words in the following discussion. Here Jung expresses concern that the doctrine of the Assumption of Mary (which he appreciated very much on other grounds) denies matter, since matter and mother are integrally related:

> The Christian "Queen of Heaven" has, obviously, shed all her Olympian qualities except for her brightness, goodness, and eternality; and even her human body, the thing most prone to gross material corruption, has put on an ethereal incorruptibility. . . . . This being so, the question naturally arises for the psychologist: what has become of the characteristic relation of the mother image to the earth, darkness, the abysmal side of the bodily man with his animal passions and instinctual nature, and to "matter" in general?[21]

Although Jung intends that "the abysmal side of the bodily man" (the material, natural, instinctual side) be understood to belong to everyone and not just to women, his use of symbolic feminine language gives the impression that women and the feminine represent the embodied side of being human. In this, Jung has ample company in Western patriarchal philosophy and Christian theology.

Given the fear, awe, and connection with matter with which Jung has endowed the anima, it is clear that opposites as strong as life and death have made their way into this image. The anima concept represents that aspect of being human which is organic, awesome, powerful, and apparently very frightening. I wonder if the fear and awe the anima evokes is due, at bottom, to "her" associations with life and death, with ultimate beginnings and endings. Although this side of being human is no more "feminine" than it is "masculine," the implications of the symbolic association of the material level and the anima, the feminine, and women are profound. Jung's intention with the anima concept was to encourage men to claim this image as part of themselves, but the symbolic feminine language functions at the same time to keep men one step removed from a full realization of their human frailty, emotionality, and vulnerability. In this way, the symbolic language of the anima functions seductively and dangerously, reinforcing men's desires to avoid the reality of male embodiment and vulnerability. If men felt these qualities fully as theirs, rather than as belonging to their animas, they would be closer to the truth. They would also be closer to feeling generally, and would be less alienated and afraid of women, the anima, and the "feminine."

Another Jungian discussion of the anima illustrates the problem of symbolic feminine language more clearly:

> The anima is a factor of the utmost importance in the psychology of a man wherever emotions and affects are at work. She intensifies, exaggerates, falsifies, and mythologizes all emotional relationships with his work and with other people of both sexes. The resultant fantasies and entanglements are all her doing. When the anima is strongly constellated, she softens the man's character and makes him touchy, irritable, moody, jealous, vain, and unadjusted. [22]

Such language mythologizes a man's difficulty integrating his emotional, affective side. Attributing the difficulties to "her," Jung seems to blame woman once again for man's troubles, even though this is the "woman within." Personifying the projection-making factor in this case as "she" takes the mythological and symbolic perspective too far.

Jung's concept of the anima represents an important first step in his recognition of a "feminine" side in men, and in the effort to enable men to come to terms with this side of themselves. Seen from a feminist perspective, his descriptions of the anima reveal the source of emotional alienation from which Western men seem to suffer. Men's fear of embodiment, vulnerability, dependency, and emotionality, all of which they have projected onto the feminine and women, functions to distort reality. Jung's anima concept allows men to recognize "the abysmal side of the bodily man" as the "feminine" part of themselves. Yet it does not go all the way to a solution for men's and women's relationships with each other, endowed as it is with misogyny and undetected fear. For every forward step out of sexism in Jung's psychology, there is at least one corresponding step backwards. In the case of the anima, Jung's psychology intersects with sexism in its deepest form: men's unconscious desires to escape the implications of their own embodiment and passions.

THE FEMININE

Jung and Jungians see the term "the feminine" as close to, but not the same thing as, the anima. "The feminine" is a short form of "the feminine principle"—a term that refers both to an archetype and to women's conscious way of being in the world. Toni Wolff, at one time Jung's analysand, later his mistress and collaborator, developed a schema representing the four archetypal forms of the feminine. Ann Ulanov has elaborated on these four forms in her book *The Feminine in Jungian Psychology and in Christian Theology*. Wolff's and Ulanov's work make up a typology, operating on the same principle as Jung's psychological types. If one draws a diagram to represent the "feminine," the four types are "opposed" to one another, represented by the four lines of the squared circle. As in Jung's typology where, for example, thinking and feeling are opposed, "Mother" and "Hetaira" are opposed, as are "Medium" and "Amazon." This opposition means that one cannot be a mother and an hetaira (soul-mate, companion) at the same time, just as one cannot be both a medium (a woman "tuned-in" to the surrounding collective unconscious) and an amazon (an independent woman) simultaneously. Every woman is supposed to have one "superior type," one or two more "functional types," and one "inferior type," exactly as in Jung's typology. The fourfoldness of the typology illustrates both tendencies of Jung's model that we discussed earlier—the potential for conflict, as well as the potential for balance. These types of the "feminine" are considered natural, characterological, and have the same connection to the sacred that we have observed in Jung's archetypal images:

> These fundamental archetypal forms of the feminine are described in the myths and legends of all cultures throughout history, as for example in the recurrent tales of the princess, the maiden, the wise woman, the witch, etc. In our everyday speech, when we decribe women we know or know about, we often resort to typing them, unconsciously using archetypal imagery. Common examples are the references to a woman as "a witch," "a man-eater," and so forth. The archetypal forms of the feminine describe certain basic ways of channeling one's feminine instincts and one's orientation to cultural factors. They also indicate the type of woman one is or the type of anima personality a man is likely to develop.[23]

Jungians often link women's conscious ways of being "feminine" to men's anima types, as Ulanov does in the quote above.

Many feminists have criticized this use of myths and legends as a base for psychology and symbolism, claiming that the myths and legends we have inherited represent patriarchal consciousness. I will point out briefly the androcentrism in the typology, which, once again, sees women's identities in terms of a relationship (or lack of relationship) to a man. Ulanov defines each of the four types in terms of the women's relationships in general and to men in particular. For example, she says the mother "relates to persons in a collective way and relates to persona in a man." The hetaira "relates to persons in an individual way, and relates to the personal unconscious and subjective anima in a man." The same relational emphasis is true for the medium and the amazon. The medium "relates to nonpersonal goals in an individual way and to the collective unconscious and objective anima in a man," and the amazon "relates to nonpersonal goals in a collective way and to the ego in a man."[24] There is the danger in this typology of "archetypalizing," that is, of reifying, social roles. Peter Berger's argument about the way religion legitimates social roles is useful here. He points out that "the cosmization of the institutions permits the individual to have an ultimate sense of rightness, both cognitively and normatively, in the roles he is expected to play in society. . . . When roles, and the institutions to which they belong, are endowed with cosmic significance, the individual's self-identification with them attains a further dimension."[25]

Elevating modes of behavior and social roles to the level of symbol contains the possibility of sanctioning women's victimization in patriarchy. The squalid life of a prostitute can, for example, take on quasi-romantic overtones and a sacred legitimation when understood in such archetypal terms. Witness Edward Whitmont's discussion of the hetaira type:

> Being given over to the concern with individual feeling, with its everchanging fluctuations, this type of woman may find it difficult to commit herself to any permanence in outer relationships. Indeed, she may, like her male counterpart, the *puer aeternus*, shy away from any concrete commitment and forever lead a provisory life of emotional wandering. The mythological images which express this type are the love deities, hierodules and priestesses dedicated to the service of love; the seductresses, nymphs, beautiful witches and harlots also express its unadapted aspect.[26]

The words "beautiful witches and harlots" may express a man's feeling for such women, but they are unlikely to capture the emotional and social reality of the woman's experience. If a prostitute were to come to a Jungian analyst's office, the analyst's goal would be to free her from an identification with the unadapted aspect of the hetaira archetypal image. The question I raise is, why archetypalize the experience of such a person in the first place? Doing so always gives a cosmic dimension to social arrangements. Unlocking, seeing-through, the linking of sexist arrangements and the sacred could be truly healing, demystifying the distortions of the patriarchal perspective writ large in social reality.

Besides considering the "feminine" as women's conscious side and as an archetypal principle, Jung conceived of the unconscious as "feminine" in general: "Psychologically the self is a union of conscious (masculine) and unconscious (feminine). It stands for the psychic totality. So formulated, it is a psychological concept."[27] As a general principle, this formulation does not work for women, and Jung did not often bother to try to square it with his statements about women's "feminine consciousness." When he did, however, he came up with absurdities that he himself recognized, as in the following passage:

> If then Luna characterizes the feminine psyche and Sol the masculine, consciousness would be an exclusively masculine

affair, which is obviously not the case since woman possesses consciousness too. But as we have previously identified Sol with consciousness and Luna with the unconscious, we would now be driven to the conclusion that a woman cannot possess a consciousness.[28]

Some other Jungians, disregarding the difficulties in pursuing the model too far, tried to take it further than Jung did. Erich Neumann asserts that "man experiences the 'masculine' structure of his conscious as peculiarly his own, and the 'feminine' unconscious as something alien to him, whereas woman feels at home in her unconscious and out of her element in consciousness."[29]

In one sense, Jung's characterization of the unconscious as "feminine" does work for women as well as for men. Since the major social institutions and modes of knowing all reflect a masculine consciousness, what has gone underground for everyone are women's perceptions, and thus the unconscious is feminine. Especially for women entering "masculine" fields, who learn the accepted mode of self-expression, the language of dominance, the unconscious would be feminine. However, as we have seen repeatedly, the Jungian way of explaining such phenomena always imparts a sense of cosmic approbation and very little, if any, social critique.

ANIMUS

Jung derived his concept of the anima from his own experience. Even though in some ways he was unable to see through his own projections, he did come up with a remarkable model for understanding men's feelings about women. We have been able to discern how men's disproportionate anima projections bear an inverse relationship to the meager power of women in patriarchal culture. The animus is another matter entirely. Jung's insistence on the model of psychic contrasexuality and his allegiance to potential balance as a main factor in the model lead to significant distortions when it comes to the animus. We have already noted Jung's complaint that women do not understand the animus as readily as men do the anima. Women's adverse reaction to his revival of the conundrum of whether or not women have souls may be one reason. Moreover, whereas Jung's descriptions of the anima connect with the experience of other men, coming as they do from his own life, his descriptions of the animus are a step removed from women's lived experience. They are, in fact, his descriptions of what it feels like to him, as a man, to see a woman in different states of mind. Naomi Goldenberg's critique of the animus as derivative is on target. Common sense tells us that Jung could not "live" the animus as he did the anima. That there are considerably more references to the anima than there are to the animus in Jung's *Collected Works* testifies to Jung's far greater personal involvement with the anima.

In my presentation of the theory of analytical psychology in chapter 4, I commented specifically on two aspects of the animus theory as it stands: its "plurality," as contrasted with the anima's "singularity," and its significance for the discussion of the female soul. Another ramification of the model of "balance" or "symmetry" enters the picture with Jung's assumption that the parent of the opposite sex is the object of an infant's first projections. That means that sons first project onto their mothers, and daughters onto their fathers. "Just as the mother seems to be the first carrier of the projection-making factor for the son, so is the father for the daughter." [30] Here Jung's insistence on the model of sexual complementarity leads him astray. Feminist studies of the effects of women's mothering in patriarchy offer an indispensable corrective to the Jungian view. These studies suggest, in Jungian terms, that all infants project at first on the mother, not the father, since they are nursed, held, changed, and cared for primarily by women. Even in the rare cases where an infant's primary caretaker is a man, the infant has spent nine months in the maternal womb. This still gives the mother a certain primacy, although such an infant would be more likely than most children to project the "primary caretaker image," with all its trust, fear of abandonment, longing, and love, on the father. Nancy Chodorow explains boys' and girls' personality development in terms of their primary relationships with their mothers:

> Women's mothering, then, produces asymmetries in the rela-
> tional experiences of girls and boys as they grow up. . . . Femi-
> nine personality comes to be based less on repression of inner
> objects, and fixed and firm splits in the ego and more on reten-

tion and continuity of external relationships. . . . Boys come to define themselves as more separate and distinct, with a greater sense of rigid ego boundaries and differentiation. The basic feminine sense of self is connected to the world, the basic masculine sense of self is separate.[31]

Feminist theorists such as Chodorow take into account the near universality of women's mothering in patriarchy, whereas Jung's allegiance to the model of sexual symmetry blinded him to this social fact and its consequences. The feminist perspective thus can shed more light on the misogyny in society than Jung's model can. If the mother is the first object of all infants' projections, this gives the mother and what is perceived as "feminine" great importance in the lives of both men and women. The experience of the mother is primary, built on touch, smell, nourishment, and the earliest experiences of self and other. No wonder later mother-images and memories have such a compelling, perhaps even primitive, quality. Becker in this sense correctly perceives that "the man is more cleanly neutral." As Dorothy Dinnerstein has pointed out, if men "mothered" infants as much as women currently do, perhaps both men and women would be perceived as "corporeal," neither one "cleanly neutral."

NEGATIVE ANIMUS

Like all archetypal images, Jung's concept of animus has both a positive and a negative pole. In his various discussions of animus, those of the "negative animus," or the "animus-possessed," woman predominate. Jung holds that "a woman possessed by the animus is always in danger of losing her femininity, her adapted feminine persona, just as a man in like circumstances runs the risk of effeminacy."[32] If used as a diagnostic tool, the term "animus-possessed" should be a neutral one. Its meaning would be, simply, that a woman has not come to terms with her animus, has not integrated "him," and therefore is at the mercy of this image. Unfortunately, however, discussions of the animus-possessed woman are neither neutral nor compassionate:

> In intellectual women the animus encourages a critical disputatiousness and would-be highbrowism, which, however, consists essentially in harping on some irrelevant weak point

and nonsensically making it the main one. Or a perfectly lucid discussion gets tangled up in the most maddening way through the introduction of a quite different and if possible, perverse point of view. Without knowing it, such women are solely intent upon exasperating the man and are, in consequence, the more completely at the mercy of the animus. "Unfortunately, I am always right," one of these creatures once confessed to me.[33]

Most intellectual women, since they live with frequent misogynist reminders about their incapacities in the realm of Logos, will not be amused or enlightened by such depictions. These descriptions reinforce internalized oppression in women rather than freeing them from it. One of the most wounding messages of patriarchy to women is that they do not think clearly. Jung's descriptions of the animus-possessed woman reinforce that message, rather than criticizing the context that has spawned whatever difficulties women may have in "thinking clearly."

"Critical disputatiousness," "highbrowism," "harping," "irrelevant," "nonsensically," "tangled," "maddening," "perverse," and "exasperating" are all emotionally laden words, suggesting that Jung was frustrated with a certain kind of emotional expression in women. In fact, the words even suggest an impotent rage. It is as if Jung chose to deal with his frustration with these "kinds" of women by labeling them "animus-possessed." From a man with as much authority and prestige as Jung, this labeling has destructive power.

Jung's term "animus-possessed woman" is analogous to Freud's labeling of certain women as "castrating." It serves the same purpose, which is to keep women subdued, "feminine," and unempowered except through whatever indirect channels for empowerment they can find in being "feminine." (Many Jungian women have claimed status and authority by becoming Jungian analysts and writing books, but such activity would be seen as the integration of the animus, and not as female thinking on its own terms.) Because the term "animus-possessed" as it is currently used is an invalidation of women, Jungians need to reconsider its usage. Jung's assumption that men and women are in equal and symmetrical relationships with their contrasexual sides involved a total lack of awareness of the oppression from which women suffer. Without giving this dimension its due, his psychology cannot be completely healing for women.

By advocating awareness of the social oppression of women, I am not suggesting that women need not be self-critical, that they are innocent and guilt-free, or incapable of doing wrong or wielding power over others in harmful ways. People with poor self-esteem can inflict great harm on others, and indeed often do. But I am pointing to the wounding effects of a misogynist society on women's self-esteem and the corresponding effect of Jung's psychology when he echoes patriarchy's attitudes. Inasmuch as Jung's psychology reinforces patriarchy's negative message to women, it only deepens their wounds. It does not heal them.

There is a more compassionate way of looking at the kind of behavior in women Jung labeled "animus-possessed," and that is by utilizing the concept of "internalized oppression." So-called animus-possession in women is a direct example of internalized oppression at work in the psyches of women. Because of the self-hater's nearly constant presence, women are victimized by internal voices that undermine their ability to think. Beleaguered by self-devastating propensities, it is not surprising that women sometimes appear "critical" or "disputatious" (as sometimes do men) in the way Jung characterized "animus-possessed women." "Animus-possession" understood as the internalization of society's invalidation of women makes some sense. As the negative pole of a cosmic principle, it does not.

POSITIVE ANIMUS

The positive animus, or the integrated animus, can help a woman focus and think clearly. If she listens to "him," "his" guidance lends her an authority and direction she will probably lack otherwise. Another of Jung's characterizations of the animus suggests "his" compensatory function clearly:

> In woman the compensating figure is of a masculine character, and can therefore appropriately be termed the *animus*. . . . Just as a woman is often clearly conscious of things which a man is still groping for in the dark, so there are naturally fields of experience in a man which, for woman, are still wrapped in the shadows of non-differentiation, chiefly things in which she has little interest. Personal relations are as a rule more important and interesting to her than objective facts and their interconnections. The wide fields of commerce, politics, technology,

and science, the whole realm of the applied masculine mind, she relegates to the penumbra of consciousness.[34]

One issue here is Jung's starting point: he assumes that a woman is not interested in "objective facts and their inter-connections." Given that "natural" deficit, she needs the "animus" to provide her with the capacity to think about such things. A second issue recalls our discussion of the anima; by conceptualizing their thinking side as masculine, women are distanced from their thinking. To be more precise, if a woman refers to her "thinking side" as "he," personifying it in Jungian fashion, she colludes with a patriarchally encouraged tendency to see only the male as rational, logical, and dependable. Just as men need to own their *male* vulnerability, dependency, and fears of embodiment, so do women need to own their *female* authority, clarity, and analytical ability and in this way challenge and help to break down patriarchal society's fear of authority in women.

In spite of these failings, Jung's psychology, including his psychology of the animus, has meant a great deal to many women. We can see that, although his starting point leaves women in a deficit position with regard to natural female authority, logic, and rationality, the schema does allow women to claim those qualities via their "masculine side." That is clearly more liberating than not claiming them at all. Furthermore, women who are attracted to Jungian psychology find an appreciation of the "feminine" in Jung's work, and often feel vindicated in a way of being that our society does not value. Jung's portrayals of the "feminine" often include receptivity, and many women feel validated by Jung's recognition of the importance of receptivity. So either way—whether by integrating their "masculine side" or by embracing the "feminine" more fully, some women have come to lead more fulfilling lives as a result of the application of Jung's theories. The fact that the "feminine" represents Jung's (and many men's) experience of what he calls "feminine" would not trouble such women because our entire society shares his androcentric perspective. Likewise, because women habitually internalize sexism, it is easy for women not to notice Jung's sexism. It is, in fact, a far more difficult task for a woman to challenge the standards of patriarchy than it is for her to actualize her "masculine" side.

Moreover, some female Jungian analysts have written about women's psychology, especially the animus, with a feeling for women's issues and experiences that Jung himself lacked. Emma Jung, his wife, is an example. Her work offers a more empathic treatment of the animus than Jung's does, probably because she allowed the animus to come forth in her own life, thereby endowing her descriptions of animus with the authority of experience—an authority visible in Jung's own depictions of anima. I am suggesting that, while Jung seems to have derived his concept of animus from his experience of anima and from his model of balance, women have corroborated Jung's animus concept by dreaming about men, fantasizing about them, and projecting their own strength, rationality, and authority onto men. It is safe to say that all people entertain contrasexual images in dreams and fantasies, since we live in a world peopled by both sexes and we dream and fantasize about this world. Therefore, as women internalized Jung's model, it was not hard to make it their own, and Jung's model found easy "verification." Emma Jung appears to have made the model her own, since she describes the animus in terms that "zero in" on women's psychological needs. She characterizes the "masculine principle" as having four main expressions: the Word, Power, Meaning, and the Deed. These potentialities are remarkably accurate—they represent areas women need to claim. Emma Jung also describes the "negative animus" in a way that most women could accept more readily than Jung's, because she deals with the internal experience of the self-hater: "First we hear from it a critical, usually negative comment on every movement, an exact examination of all motives and intentions, which naturally always causes feelings of inferiority, and tends to nip in the bud all initiative and every wish for self-expression."[35] Had she located these remarks within the context of patriarchy, which encourages women's "negative comments on every movement," Emma Jung would have added the dimension needed to heal women's self-images more fully. From her description of the animus's critical propensities, she goes on to say that "from time to time, this same voice may also dispense exaggerated praise, and the result of these extremes of judgment is that one oscillates to and fro between the consciousness of complete futility and a blown-up sense of one's own value and importance."[36]

Emma Jung bases this insight on Jung's concept of polarity in all the archetypal images. Swinging from negative to positive evaluations by the animus, a woman's only healthy alternative is to "befriend" this voice and to make "his" insights her own, thus "taming him" somewhat. Again, Emma Jung's psychology of women would have been enhanced had she realized that bouncing back and forth between negative and positive evaluations replicates men's images of women in patriarchy. "Split" images of women are daily fare in patriarchy—by "split," I mean polarized between "bad" and "good," as in the well-known madonna/whore split. Women internalize these polarized images, experiencing themselves in exaggerated terms as "good" and "bad," "wholly responsible" or "not responsible at all."

Beneficial uses of Jung's concept of the animus, like the anima, will necessarily involve seeing how these images reflect their patriarchal context. De-ontologized and contextualized, Jung's anima and animus can be useful to women and men. By "de-ontologized," I mean removing the dimension of the Sacred, ever-lurking behind these archetypal images. By "contextualized," I mean seeing them in relation to their social context, as I have attempted to see them here—a departure from the usual Jungian presentation. Everybody has emotionally powerful images of other people in dreams and fantasies. Jung's suggestion of dialogue with and integration of these images is a creative and workable way of acknowledging and even transforming one's inner dynamics. However, as I have pointed out, these images need to shed the potential they now carry for legitimation of patriarchal society's fear and devaluation of women.

My criticism of sexist elements in Jung's thought is not meant to disparage his very real contribution to human self-understanding. Especially appealing in Jung is his emphasis on the spiritual dimension of life. For spiritual seekers, his view is like water in the arid desert of psychologies based solely on the "material" view of human beings. Jung was driven by the deepest questions spiritual seekers have always posed, and he was not afraid of asking those questions as a psychologist. In his own use of the term, he approached these issues "empirically," using himself as the subject and object of his own experiment. Jung's spiritual quest led him beyond the level of the merely "material" to wrestle with dualities and oppositions in human life. In his later years, he ventured beyond traditional Western epistemology by positing that "spirit" and "matter" are in some sense one. In the same manner, he challenged the subject/object split and the delusion of "pure objectivity" characteristic of Western philosophical dualism. Seeking to bring together perspectives from East and West, Jung was a pioneer in a holistic psychology of the self and of nations. And finally, he wrestled with the problem of evil all his life. Even if his theology is unclear, and perhaps based in unresolved anger at his father and his father's Father, no one can claim that Jung spared himself the hard questions.

For all its faults from the point of view of women's search for authentic self-definitions, arising out of their own lives and woman-affirming experience, Jung's valuing of what he called the "feminine" has pointed to what is lacking, undervalued, misunderstood, and feared in the Western world. The next step for Jungians is to step back and allow the "feminine" to arise out of women's experience, not imposing on this term, or on women, Jung's ambivalence or the culture- and gender-based limitations of his perspective.

I have already suggested some reasons why Jungians can easily miss the misogyny in Jungian psychology. We have discussed his high valuing of the "feminine," as well as the veneration in which most Jungians hold Jung—a veneration that makes criticism difficult, if not impossible. A final factor—one we examined in some depth in chapter 2—is that in Western patriarchy, misogynist interpretations of women constitute the fabric of their self-images. We have all become so habituated to misogyny and androcentrism in patriarchy that until the recent advent of feminism we have not noticed them. Partly as a result of this habituation, and even more deeply because of fear of violating socially agreed upon codes, for women to cast aside misogyny and the corresponding habit of self-hatred is extremely difficult, but very important to begin nonetheless. Since living with misogyny is a constant in women's lives, a psychological model, to be adequate and healing, must take it into account. In a coalition with feminism, which provides the analytical tools to unmask sexism and misogyny in society and in women's psyches, Jung's psychology can provide a more accurate map of our "inner" world and its relation to the "outer" world than it can alone. With his unexamined acceptance of male-generated gender-related images, Jung has dealt primarily with the inner world of the male and its projections.

The sociology of knowledge that has served as a methodological "lens" in this book tends to "flatten" reality. While it is a helpful methodology—especially as it is allied with feminism—its sociological reductionism leaves many dimensions of life unexplored. The sociology of knowledge as a worldview is particularly impoverished in an area where Jung's psychology is rich, the area of spirituality. Jung's emphasis on the reality of our deepest spiritual questions, as well as on the experiential and the nonrational, presents an insistent corrective to Western society's materialism. Correcting the fear of women and the feminine, encased even within Jung's efforts to validate the feminine, will be an essential step toward making Jung's the holistic psychology and spirituality women need it to be.

NOTES

CHAPTER ONE

1. Hans Dieckmann, *Twice-Told Tales: The Psychological Use of Fairy Tales,* Foreword by Bruno Bettelheim, trans. Boris Matthews (Wilmette, Ill.: Chiron Publications, 1986), vii–viii.

2. Ibid., viii.

3. For the outcome of this insight for the young woman, see Bettelheim's account (ibid., ix).

4. Ann Ulanov, *Receiving Woman: Studies in the Psychology and Theology of the Feminine* (Philadelphia: Westminster Press, 1981), 17.

5. Ibid., 44.

6. Ibid., 73–74.

7. Rosemary Ruether, *Sexism and God-Talk: Toward a Feminist Theology* (Boston: Beacon Press, 1983), 190.

8. Ibid.

9. Mary Daly, *Gyn/Ecology: The Metaethics of Radical Feminism* (Boston: Beacon Press, 1978), 280.

10. June Singer and Stephanie Halpern, "Two Responses to Naomi Goldenberg," *Anima* 4, no. 1 (Fall Equinox 1977): 59–61.

11. Ibid., 61.

12. C. G. Jung, *Collected Works,* ed. Sir Herbert Read, Michael Fordham, and Gerhard Adler; trans. R. F. C. Hull, Bollingen Series 20 (Princeton: Princeton University Press, 1904), 8:133. This term, like other Jungian terms, is explained in more depth in chapter 3.

13. Estella Lauter and Carol Schreier Rupprecht, *Feminist Archetypal*

Theory: Interdisciplinary Re-Visions of Jungian Thought (Knoxville: University of Tennessee Press, 1985), 236.

14. See Naomi Goldenberg, "Archetypal Theory after Jung," *Spring: An Annual of Archetypal Psychology and Jungian Thought* (1975): 199–220; "A Feminist Critique of Jung," *Signs: Journal of Women in Culture and Society* 2, no. 2 (1976): 443–49; "Feminism and Jungian Theory," *Anima* 3, no. 2 (Spring Equinox 1977): 14–18; and Carol Christ, "Some Comments on Jung, Jungians, and the Study of Women," *Anima* 3, no. 2 (Spring Equinox 1977): 66–69. Some Jungian responses to Christ and Goldenberg can be found in *Anima* 4, no. 1 (Fall Equinox 1977).

15. Christ, "Some Comments," 68.

16. Naomi Goldenberg, *Changing of the Gods: Feminism and the End of Traditional Religions* (Boston: Beacon Press, 1979). See chapter 5, pp. 48–72.

17. Goldenberg, *Changing of the Gods,* 57–58.

18. Compare these two positions:

> Patriarchy is itself the prevailing religion of the entire planet, and its essential message is necrophilia. All of the so-called religions legitimating patriarchy are mere sects subsumed under its vast umbrella/canopy. . . . All—from buddhism and hinduism to islam, judaism, christianity, to secular derivatives such as freudianism, jungianism, marxism and maoism—are infrastructures of the edifice of patriarchy. All are erected as parts of the male's shelter against anomie. Consequently, women are the objects of male terror, the projected personifications of "The Enemy," the real objects under attack in all the wars of patriarchy. (Mary Daly, *Gyn/Ecology,* 39)

Anthropologist Peggy Sanday, speaking of the work of feminist anthropologists making claims similar to Daly's, says:

> Because the matriarchy theory has been resurrected as a historical fact by contemporary feminists, anthropologists have searched for societies in which women have publicly recognized power and authority surpassing that of men. Finding no society in which women occupy the main positions of leadership, anthropologists argue that male dominance is universal.
>
> There is a certain bias to this point of view, a bias that is understandable given the Western equation of dominance with public leadership. By defining dominance differently, one can show that in many societies male leadership is balanced by female authority. (Peggy Reeves Sanday, *Female Power and Male Dominance: On the Origins of Sexual Inequality* [Cambridge: Cambridge University Press, 1981], 113)

19. There are also some feminists who hold to the innate differences theory. These feminists in some ways come close to Jungian psychology. They value the "feminine" highly and think that Jung described the differences between the sexes correctly. For example, see *Moon, Moon,* by Anne Kent Rush (New York and Berkeley: Random House and Moon Books, 1976).

20. The wide variety of intrasexual differences that have been observed throughout cultures does, at this point, corroborate the social constructionist school.

21. Significant works documenting these dangers are those of Mary Daly and Rosemary Ruether. See also *Womanspirit Rising,* edited by Carol Christ and Judith Plaskow (San Francisco: Harper and Row, 1979).

22. In the Introduction to *Black Rage* by William H. Grier and Price M. Cobbs (New York: Basic Books, Harper Colophon Books, 1968) is a passionate paragraph underscoring the need for therapy with blacks to recognize racism as a fact and to oppose it "in an unrelenting way." The rightness of this so struck me that I changed "racism" to "sexism" and adopted this criterion as a guideline for therapy with women.

CHAPTER TWO

1. See Peter Berger, *The Sacred Canopy: Elements of a Sociological Theory of Religion* (Garden City, N.Y.: Doubleday and Co., 1967).

2. In a letter to Miss Sally M. Pinckney of September 30, 1948, Jung said the following regarding the individual's need for a group:

> Although the dangers of the individual identifying with the collectivity are very great indeed, the relationship between these two factors is not necessarily negative. It has its very positive aspects too. As a matter of fact a positive relationship between the individual and society or a group is essential, since no individual stands by himself but depends upon symbiosis with a group. The self, the very centre of an individual, is of a conglomerate nature. It is, as it were, a group. It is a collectivity in itself and therefore always, when it works most positively, creates a group. (C. G. Jung, *Letters,* ed. Gerhard Adler and Aniela Jaffe [Princeton: Princeton University Press, 1973], 1:508)

Jung's emphasis, however, is still different from that of the social psychologists or the sociologists of knowledge, since he conceives of the conglomerate nature of the self (archetype) expressing itself in a collectivity. The archetype is still primary. Moreover, what Jung describes in this letter is different from his more frequently voiced concern, which is that the individual will be "swallowed up" by group forces and lose his or her individuality.

3. Jung addresses this necessity with his concept of animus development in women. I will define this term in chapter 4, along with other Jungian concepts, and will discuss it from a feminist perspective in chapter 6.

4. See Vivian Gornick and Barbara K. Moran, eds., *Woman in Sexist Society: Studies in Power and Powerlessness* (New York: Basic Books, 1971); and Inge Broverman et al., "Sex-Role Stereotypes: A Current Appraisal," *Journal of Social Issues* 18, no. 2 (1972).

5. Simone de Beauvoir, *The Second Sex* (New York: Vintage Books, 1974; copyright by Librairie Gallimard, 1949).

6. Mary Daly's discussion of tokenism in *Gyn/Ecology* is one of the best.

7. Examples of androcentrism in scholarship abound. They are so prevalent that one can find them in almost any nonfeminist book. For example, see the first nineteen pages of Freud's *The Future of an Illusion.* Women will be more likely to notice the jarring shift in the meaning of the words "men," "man," "people," and "one" than men will, since men remain the subject of these words. Women shift in and out of subjecthood; first they are included, it seems, as part of "man," or "men," as is usual in generic masculine language. Abruptly, the use of these words changes to mean *males* only, so that one wonders if women were really included in the terms before. The realization dawns that women were not included in what preceded either. Indeed, the entire transaction Freud is talking about is taking place between *men*. The exclusiveness of male "inclusive" language has been amply noted by many feminists, especially by Mary Daly in the United States and by the French feminists.

8. "Minorities," a term sometimes applied to blacks and to women, obviously does not mean "minority" in the sense of numbers. White people are in the minority worldwide, and women are in the majority. However, the word "minority" has a purpose since it designates diminished authority and exclusion from the norm.

9. One of the best such discussions is that of Carol Christ and Judith Plaskow in the introduction to *Womanspirit Rising.*

10. Polly Young-Eisendrath, "New Contexts and Conversations for Female Authority" (Paper presented at "Feminist Thought and the Structure of Knowledge," Colloquium for Social Philosophy, Pennsylvania State University, Delaware County Campus, April 19, 1986), p. 4.

11. I will not discuss the phenomenon of worshipping women, of elevating them to a position of greater purity and goodness than men—a phenomenon particularly characteristic of the nineteenth century—except to say that it is the other side of the coin of devaluation. Neither exaltation nor devaluation serves the purpose of helping women to attain full personhood, although clearly the former carries greater appeal for women themselves than does the latter. This positive/negative split in images of women shows how little patriarchy has integrated women into its institutions and consciousness. If women were integrated into society fully, the images would not be split.

12. Carol Christ has commented extensively on Lessing's vision and its importance, and on the fact that, although it is spiritual, it need not be seen as antithetical to politics. See Christ's discussions of Martha Quest in *Womanspirit Rising* and in *Diving Deep and Surfacing: Women Writers on Spiritual Quest* (Boston: Beacon Press, 1980).

13. By the use of the terms "inner figure" or "inner voice," I am not locating the source of the figure or voice within. I see them as images internalized from a patriarchal context, which, among other things, goes so far as to credit women with the existence of evil in the world. Within everyone, I imagine, and certainly within women, there exists the propensity to "carry the projection" as Jungians say—that is, to be the person one is assumed to be by significant others in the ongoing, nomizing conversation.

14. Doris Lessing, *The Four-Gated City* (New York: Bantam Books, 1969), 518–19.

15. Ibid., 535.

16. Mary Daly, *Pure Lust: Elemental Feminist Philosophy* (Boston: Beacon Press, 1984), 139.

17. Jean Baker Miller, *Toward a New Psychology of Women* (Boston: Beacon Press, 1976), 7.

18. Ibid., 11.

19. Daly, *Gyn/Ecology*, 337.

20. Ibid., 377.

21. Nelle Morton, "Beloved Image" (Paper presented to the American Academy of Religion, December 28, 1977), 19.

22. Carol Christ, "Why Women Need the Goddess: Phenomenological, Psychological and Political Reflections," *Womanspirit Rising*, 274.

23. For the following analysis of religion's role in legitimizing social structures, codes, and rules, I rely on Peter Berger's work in *The Sacred Canopy*.

24. Berger, *The Sacred Canopy*, 32.

25. This is not to say that a society with feminine symbols for the Divine will necessarily recognize women's social power any more than will a society with only masculine symbols. Hinduism, for example, has feminine and masculine divine imagery, but in the Hindu religion and society women are still subordinate to men. The issue of religious symbolism and social authority is complicated, since male social power and public authority seem to be so widely respected and expected. However, for women raised in a religious tradition with only masculine imagery for the Divine, the restoration of feminine imagery to the Godhead is one way of enhancing their self-respect and their sense of empowerment.

CHAPTER THREE

1. In *Psychology and Religion: West and East*, Jung writes: "It is almost an absurd prejudice to suppose that existence can only be physical. As a matter of fact, the only form of existence of which we have immediate knowledge is psychic. We might well say, on the contrary, that

physical existence is a mere inference, since we know of matter only in so far as we perceive psychic images mediated by the senses." (*Collected Works*, 11 : 12).

Yet, of course, Jung was not a true Platonist, nor an Idealist, nor was he philosophically rigorous. His true intent (which became clearer later in his life) was to go beyond dualism—which would mean going beyond Plato's real world of ideas versus the shadowy world of form— to a worldview that would embrace both sides of the opposition, and all things as real.

2. C. G. Jung, *Memories, Dreams, Reflections* (New York: Random House, Vintage Books, 1961), 3.

3. See Andrew Samuels, *Jung and the Post-Jungians* (London: Routledge and Kegan Paul, 1985) for an excellent treatment of the prominent figures in Jungian psychology today and the directions they have taken theoretically and clinically.

4. See, for examples, Edward Glover, *Freud or Jung?* (London: Allen and Unwin, 1950); Paul J. Stern, *C. G. Jung: The Haunted Prophet* (New York: Braziller, 1976); Philip Rieff, *The Triumph of the Therapeutic: Uses of Faith after Freud* (New York: Harper and Row, Harper Torchbooks, 1966). Of these three, Rieff's is by far the most important critique.

5. Contrast these statements. Laurens Van der Post, in the prologue to his book, begins: "I have, I believe, known many of those the world considered great, but Carl Gustav Jung is almost the only one of whose greatness I am certain" (*Jung and the Story of Our Time*, [New York: Random House, Pantheon Books, 1975], 3). Paul Stern argues at greater length:

> From early adolescence, Carl Jung was haunted by a sense of prophetic mission. The prophet, in his eyes, was chosen through the agency of "fate" to proclaim a new truth or reestablish an ancient, forgotten one. His own prophetic revelation was that of the Reality of the Soul.
>
> On the face of it, Jung's prophetic message had the earmarks of an anachronism. By 1900, the notion of soul had been pretty much excised from the minds and vocabularies of most Western intellectuals. To promulgate, in the solemn tone peculiar to Jung, "the timeless and spaceless reality of the human soul" must have struck most of his colleagues as rather quixotic, if they paid any heed to the message at all. Nor were the Protestant (and Catholic) theologians, who were Jung's real intended audience, more likely to hail an opaque doctrine that amounted to a deification of the Self. To complain, as Jung ceaselessly did, that his message was not appreciated or fell upon deaf ears was to evince a remarkable social blindness.
>
> It was Carl Jung's misfortune to have lived at a historic juncture that was not quite ready for his gospel of inwardness. He so wanted to be a seer honored in his own time, but he had to disguise himself as a scientist. . . .
>
> While Carl Jung was without question endowed with the requisite

depth of pathology, it may have been the wrong kind for his time and place. . . .

While Jung's own descent into the psychic netherworld was less self-propelled than he liked to think, he was bold and wily enough to ultimately consent to the inevitable and thus gain a foothold in a new larger reality. (*Jung,* 6, 7, 8)

I am grateful to Christine Downing who was my first teacher of depth psychology. Her balanced presentation of Freud and Jung allowed them to shed light on one another, rather than furthering the usual polarization and tension between the two.

6. Homans believes that Jung's attitude toward Christianity contains at the same time a "hermeneutics of affirmation" and a "hermeneutics of suspicion." He argues that Jung reinterprets traditional Christianity, not that he rejects it altogether. See Peter Homans, *Jung in Context: Modernity and the Making of a Psychology* (Chicago: University of Chicago Press, 1979).

7. I exclude such obvious universals as the human need to care for and provide for one's young, to find food for one's social group, and to secure protection from danger.

8. Jung, *Memories,* 50.

9. See *Memories* for a complete report, and his doctoral dissertation, "On the Psychology and Pathology of So-Called Occult Phenomena" (*Collected Works,* 1:3–88), for an example. Jung's dissertation was a study of his young cousin, a medium, in which he attempted to understand paranormal states of consciousness.

10. Jung, *Memories,* 105.

11. Ibid., 106.

12. See Aldo Carotenuto, *A Secret Symmetry: Sabina Spielrein between Jung and Freud,* trans. Arno Pomerans, John Shepley, and Krishna Winston (New York: Random House, Pantheon Books, 1982).

13. Jung, *Memories,* 86.

14. Here is the dream: "It was night in some unknown place, and I was making slow and painful headway against a mighty wind. Dense fog was flying along everywhere. I had my hands cupped around a tiny light which threatened to go out at any moment. Everything depended on my keeping this little light alive. Suddenly I had the feeling that something was coming up behind me. I looked back, and saw a gigantic black figure following me. But at the same moment I was conscious, in spite of my terror, that I must keep my little light going through night and wind, regardless of all dangers. When I awoke, I realised at once that the figure was a 'specter of the Brocken,' my own shadow on the swirling mists, brought into being by the little light I was carrying. I knew, too, that this little light was my consciousness, the only light I have. My own understanding is the sole treasure I possess, and the greatest. Though infinitely small and frag-

ile in comparison with the powers of darkness, it is still a light, my only light" (*Memories,* 87–88).

15. Ibid., 88.
16. Ibid., 108–9.
17. Ibid., 109.
18. See Jung, *Collected Works,* 8:51–52.
19. Jung, *Memories,* 36.
20. Ibid., 37–40. On March 21, 1981, I attended a lecture given at the Pennsylvania Institute in Philadelphia by Professor Barry Schlochower. The lecture was entitled, "Jung's Homoerotic Attachment to Freud and Answer to Job." Schlochower analyzed Jung's cathedral fantasy as a first masturbation fantasy. He relied a great deal for his interpretation on the "bliss" and "relief" Jung experienced after letting the fantasy conclude. Anyone acquainted with Jung knows that this interpretation is false. Jung was a very private man. If, indeed, his first masturbation had accompanied this fantasy, he would not have disclosed the fantasy. Knowledge of Jung's life-long religious preoccupations, for which there are other explanations besides the sexual, indicates that the cathedral fantasy is a clear revelation of many of the religious themes that Jung would spend the rest of his life trying to elucidate.
21. For the opposition between creeds and religion, see especially Jung's *Psychology and Religion: West and East* (*Collected Works,* vol. 11) and *The Undiscovered Self* (*Collected Works,* vol. 10). In the latter he wrote:

> A creed gives expression to a definite collective belief, whereas the word *religion* expresses a subjective relationship to certain metaphysical, extramundane factors. A creed is a confession of faith intended chiefly for the world at large and is thus an intramundane affair, while the meaning and purpose of religion lie in the relationship of the individual to God (Christianity, Judaism, Islam) or to the path of salvation and liberation (Buddhism). (pp. 256–57)

22. Jung, *Memories,* 53.
23. Ibid., 55.
24. Ibid.
25. Ibid., 93.
26. Ibid., 73.
27. Jung, *Collected Works,* 3:4.
28. In a letter to Jung on April 16, 1909, Freud said: "It is remarkable that on the same evening that I formally adopted you as an eldest son, anointing you as my successor and crown prince—*in partibus infidelium*—that then and there you should have divested me of my paternal dignity, and that the divesting seems to have given you as much pleasure as investing your person gave me." (Quoted in *Memories,* 361.)
29. Jung, *Memories,* 158.
30. William McGuire, ed., *The Freud/Jung Letters: The Correspondence*

between Sigmund Freud and C. G. Jung, Bollingen Series, 94 (Princeton: Princeton University Press, 1974), 293–94.

31. Ibid., 298.

32. Jung, *Memories,* 157.

33. Sigmund Freud, *The Future of an Illusion* (Garden City, N.Y.: Doubleday, Anchor Books, 1927), 92.

34. Sigmund Freud, *The History of the Psychoanalytic Movement* (New York: Crowell-Collier, Collier Books, 1963), 93.

35. Jung, *Memories,* 170. Peter Homans analyzes this interestingly. See chapter 5 of *Jung in Context.*

36. Ibid., 130.

37. If one could examine all of Jung's formulations about his model chronologically (difficult because of the usual thematic arrangement), one might find that the dualism/conflict elements prevail during the earlier years, and the resolution/balance elements during the later ones. A fact that argues against this possibility, however, is that both tendencies are present in the typology, an early work (1918). What is clear is that Jung's leanings toward nondualism were stronger and clearer in the latter part of his life and writings.

38. Jung, *Collected Works,* 16:305.

39. Ibid., 14:497.

40. Ibid., 8:53.

41. Ibid., 26.

42. Jung, *Letters,* 2:297.

43. Ibid., 304.

44. Jung, *Collected Works,* 8:51–52.

45. Ibid., 6:509.

46. Ibid., 59.

47. Ibid., 14:89.

48. Ibid., 170–171.

CHAPTER FOUR

1. Individuation can be seen to reflect our predominant patriarchal mythos in that Jung's ideal of the individuated person recalls Western notions of the solitary journey required of the cultural hero. The patriarchal myth of individualism and separateness (not necessarily the same as individuation—that is more complicated) is one of Western society's most harmful illusions, preventing us from experiencing our essential interdependence. For a criticism of this prevailing mythos, see Polly Young-Eisendrath and Demaris Wehr, "The Fallacy of Individualism and Reasonable Violence against Women," forthcoming in *Christianity, Patriarchy and Abuse,* ed. Carole Bohn and Joanne Brown (Philadelphia: Pilgrim Press, 1987).

2. Jung, *Collected Works,* 3:150.

3. Jung, *Memories,* 401.
4. Ibid., 401–2.
5. Ibid., 9(1):79ff.
6. Ibid., 8:213.
7. Ibid., 77–79.
8. Ibid.
9. Ibid., 3:150.
10. James Hillman, who coined the term the "little people" and suggested "befriending" them, believes that polytheistic elements are present in Jung's view of the psyche, although it is Hillman himself who draws them out explicitly. Hillman bemoans the monotheistic emphasis that the centrality of the self represents. See *Re-Visioning Psychology* (New York: Harper and Row, Harper Colophon Books, 1975) and Hillman's Appendix to David L. Miller, *The New Polytheism: Rebirth of the Gods and Goddesses* (Dallas: Spring Publications, 1981). Miller's work expands on this theme.
11. Quoted in Ann Ulanov, *The Feminine in Jungian Psychology and in Christian Theology* (Evanston: Northwestern University Press, 1979), 28.
12. Jung, *Collected Works,* 6:425.
13. Ibid., 7:201.
14. Ibid., 58–59.
15. Ibid., 9(1):122ff.
16. Jung, *Collected Works,* 7:194.
17. Edward Whitmont, *The Symbolic Quest: Basic Concepts of Analytical Psychology* (Princeton: Princeton University Press, 1969), 159.
18. Ibid., 238–39.
19. Jung, *Collected Works,* 10:280–81.
20. Ibid., 7:96.
21. Ibid., 189.
22. Ibid., 9(2):14.
23. Ibid., 10:41.
24. Jolande Jacobi, *The Psychology of C. G. Jung: An Introduction with Illustrations* (New Haven: Yale University Press, 1943), 117.
25. Jung, *Collected Works,* 7:238.
26. Ibid., 6:425.
27. Ibid., 9(2):31.
28. Ibid., 42.
29. Ibid., 16:321.
30. Ibid., 261. An impressive account of a male analyst and a female patient's holding to the symbolic and transformative elements of this level of encounter, by acknowledging the erotic dimension but not acting on it, can be found in Nathan Schwartz-Salant's essay "On the Subtle-Body Concept in Clinical Practice," *Chiron: A Review of Jungian Analysis* (Wilmette, Ill.: Chiron Publications, 1986), 19–58.
31. Ibid., 262.
32. Ibid., 263.

33. Ibid.
34. Ibid., 313.
35. Jung, *Collected Works,* 7:239–40.
36. Jung, *Memories,* 345–46.
37. Joseph Campbell, *The Portable Jung* (New York: Viking Press, 1971), 426.
38. Jung, *Collected Works,* 11:5.
39. Ibid., 6:306.
40. Ibid., 11:6.
41. Ibid., 303.
42. Ibid., 12.
43. Ian G. Barbour, *Issues in Science and Religion* (New York: Harper and Row, Harper Torchbooks, 1971), 142.
44. Jung, *Collected Works,* 11:5.
45. Ibid., 306.
46. Ibid., 7:240.

CHAPTER FIVE

1. Clifford A. Brown, *Jung's Hermenutic of Doctrine: Its Theological Significance,* A.A.R. Dissertation Series, no. 32 (Chico, Cal.: Scholars Press, 1981). See chapter 1.
2. Quoted in James Heisig, *Imago Dei: A Study of C. G. Jung's Psychology of Religion* (Lewisburg, Pa.: Bucknell U.P., 1979), 44.
3. Ibid., 113n.
4. Ibid., 114.
5. Ibid., 198.
6. "Of course God is the 'wholly Other'; but He is also the wholly Same, the wholly Present. Of course He is the Mysterium Tremendum that appears and overthrows; but He is also the mystery of the self-evident, nearer to me than my I" (Martin Buber, *I and Thou,* 2d ed., trans. R. G. Smith [New York: Scribner's, 1958], 79). Maurice Friedman pointed this passage out to me. He further elucidated Buber's position: "[Buber is critical of] the translation of all transcendence into immanence by reducing God, for all practical purposes, from the meeter that is met to the archetypal image within, met, to be sure, as other and numinous but not the otherness of what is, in fact, outside of the self, whether with a small 's' or a capital 's'" (Friedman, personal correspondence, February 26, 1986).
7. Martin Buber, *Eclipse of God: Studies in the Relation between Religion and Philosophy* (New York: Harper and Bros., 1952), 83–84.
8. Goldenberg, *Changing of the Gods,* 48.
9. Homans, *Jung in Context,* 191–92.
10. Ibid.
11. Jung, *Collected Works,* 11:7–8 (emphasis mine).

12. Ibid., 62.

13. Ibid., 43.

14. Ibid., 341.

15. Ibid., 334.

16. Frederick Streng, *Understanding Religious Man* (Belmont, Cal.: Dickenson Pub. Co., 1969), 4. Similarly, Thomas Luckmann calls religion "symbolic self-transcendence" in *The Invisible Religion: The Problem of Religion in Modern Society* (New York: Macmillan, 1967).

17. Jung, *Memories,* 173.

18. Jung, *The Undiscovered Self,* in *Collected Works,* 10:256.

19. This topic is covered in great detail in James Heisig's book *Imago Dei,* to which I refer the reader for a thorough and chronological treatment.

20. Jung, *Memories,* 303.

21. Ibid., 337.

22. Jung, *Collected Works,* 11:303.

23. Because of such statements, Jung has been called a "modern Gnostic," in particular by Maurice Friedman. See Friedman's work *To Deny Our Nothingness: Contemporary Images of Man* (New York: Dell Publishing, 1967), part 6, "The Modern Gnostic."

With respect to the enigmatic statement on the B.B.C. film, Jung said:

> I do know that I am obviously confronted with a factor unknown in itself, which I call "God" *in consensu omnium (quod semper, quod ubique, quod ab omnibus creditur).* I remember Him, I evoke Him, whenever I use his name, overcome by anger or by fear, whenever I involuntarily say: "Oh God." That happens when I meet somebody or something stronger than myself. It is an apt name given to all overpowering emotions in my own psychic system, subduing my conscious will and usurping control over myself. This is the name by which I designate all things which cross my wilful path violently and recklessly, all things which upset my subjective views, plans, and intentions and change the course of my life for better or worse. In accordance with tradition I call the power of fate in this positive as well as negative aspect, and in-asmuch as its origin is beyond my control, "God," a "personal God," since my fate means very much myself. (Jung, *Letters,* 2:571)

24. Jung, *Letters,* 2:156.

25. Jung, *Collected Works,* 11:456.

26. Ibid., 383. Antonio Moreno points out that Jung has misrepresented the Augustinian understanding of evil as *privatio boni* in any case.

> Jung's interpretation of the definition of evil as *privatio boni* is incorrect. Neither St. Augustine nor St. Thomas can deny the existence of so manifest a fact of experience. Evil is very real in the universe; and in man, evil exists: "On the assumption that evil does not exist," Aquinas says, "all prohibitions and penalties would be meaningless, for they

exist only to hold back evil. . . . Hence it is clear that evil is found in things, as corruption also is found. . ."

Evil therefore exists; it is real, very real. . . . Therefore Augustine's definition of evil cannot be an excuse for denying its existence—and even less for justifying morally reprehensible practices, or any other consequences that follow as a result of erroneous interpretations of that definition. . . . Evil exists, but with what kind of existence? . . . Good and evil are opposites, but of what kind is the opposition corresponding to them? (Antonio Moreno, *Jung, Gods, and Modern Man* [Notre Dame, Ind.: University of Notre Dame Press, 1970], 151–54)

27. Jung, *Collected Works*, 11:419.
28. Ibid., 183.
29. Ibid., 468.
30. Heisig, *Imago Dei*, 26.
31. Ibid., 137.
32. Jung, *Collected Works*, 11:469.
33. Ibid., 10:483.
34. Jung, *Letters*, 2:260.
35. Jung, *Collected Works*, 11:459.
36. Heisig, *Imago Dei*, 126.
37. Jung, *Letters*, 2:156.
38. Jolande Jacobi, *Complex, Archetype, Symbol in the Psychology of C. G. Jung*, 31.
39. Jung, *Collected Works*, 1:160.
40. Jung, *Letters*, 2:23.
41. Ibid., 258.
42. Jung, *Collected Works*, 11:275.
43. Ibid., 204.
44. Ibid., 7:77.
45. Ibid., 234.
46. Ibid., 11:15.
47. Homans, *Jung in Context*, 190–91.
48. Goldenberg, *Changing of the Gods*, 25.
49. Greenberg and Mitchell provide a helpful discussion of current thinking in the philosophy of science on pp. 16–19 of their book, *Object Relations in Psychoanalytic Theory* (Cambridge: Harvard University Press, 1983). I include part of it here.

Contemporary philosophers of science have reconsidered the relationship between science and "objective" reality. There are no purely objective facts and observations which lie outside of theory, according to this new view. One's theory, one's understanding, one's way of thinking, *determine* what are likely to be taken as facts, determine how and what one observes. Observation itself is understood to be "theory-laden."

With regard to Thomas Kuhn's work, they say:

Paradigms, because they are models of reality taken for the "truth" inspire loyalties. During the peak period of influence of a paradigm, nearly all workers within the particular field are under its sway. There is shared agreement on the epistemological assumptions, the methodological approaches, and the observational perimeter which it provides. As that peak period is passed, new data, new ideas begin to emerge outside the boundaries legitimized by the paradigm. At that point an array of different strategic options presents itself. Some remain loyal to the old paradigm and discount the validity of new, discordant data and concepts altogether. Another strategy, which might be termed accommodation, entails attempts to stretch the concepts and boundaries of the old paradigm to encompass what is new.

With regard to psychoanalytic models:

Psychoanalytic theories operate as models reflecting metaphysical commitments because they are based upon untestable premises.

50. Jung, *Collected Works*, 17 : 198.

CHAPTER SIX

1. See James Hillman, *Anima: An Anatomy of a Personified Notion* (Dallas: Spring Publications, 1985); Irene de Castillejo, *Knowing Woman* (New York: Harper and Row, 1973); Edward Whitmont, "Reassessing Femininity and Masculinity: A Critique of Some Traditional Assumptions," *Quadrant* 13, no. 2 (Fall 1980). At least four contemporary Jungian analysts have written theoretical works with feminist concerns. These are Linda Leonard, *The Wounded Woman: Healing the Father-Daughter Relationship* (Boston: Shambala Books, 1982); Sylvia Brinton Perera, *Descent to the Goddess: A Way of Initiation for Women* (Toronto: Inner City Books, 1981); Jean Shinoda Bolen, *Goddesses in Everywoman: A New Psychology of Women* (San Francisco: Harper and Row, 1984), and Polly Young-Eisendrath, *Hags and Heroes: A Feminist Approach to Jungian Psychotherapy with Couples* (Toronto: Inner City Books, 1984). Of these four, Bolen and Young-Eisendrath are the most avowedly feminist, discussing their experience with feminism as part of their own awakening and as informing their work as Jungian analysts.
2. See Lauter and Rupprecht, *Feminist Archetypal Theory;* see also Catherine Keller, "Wholeness in the King's Men," *Anima* 11, no. 2 (Spring Equinox 1985): 83-95.
3. Jung addressed the issue of those who do not have sufficient ego strength to enter the depths of unconscious experience, experience that might induce a latent psychosis to become manifest. He did not consider the possibility of women's egos being different and less firmly fixed than men's, however, nor the possibility that "annihilation" of the ego would therefore be inappropriate for women.
Judith Plaskow and Valerie Saiving are two feminist theologians

who have written about the inadequacy for women of traditional definitions of sin. Saiving says:

> For the temptations of woman *as woman* are not the same as the temptations of man *as man,* and the specifically feminine forms of sin—"feminine" not because they are confined to women or because women are incapable of sinning in other ways but because they are outgrowths of the basic feminine character structure—have a quality which can never be encompassed by such terms as "pride" and "will-to-power." They are better suggested by such items as triviality, distractibility, and diffuseness; lack of an organizing center or focus; dependence on others for one's own self-definition; tolerance at the expense of standards of excellence; inability to respect the boundaries of privacy; sentimentality, gossipy sociability, and mistrust of reason—in short, underdevelopment or negation of the self. ("The Human Situation," *Womanspirit Rising,* 37).

See also Judith Plaskow, *Sex, Sin, and Grace: Women's Experience and the Theologies of Reinhold Niebuhr and Paul Tillich* (Lanham, Md.: University Press of America, 1980).

4. Miller, *Toward a New Psychology of Women,* 72.

5. Nancy Chodorow, *The Reproduction of Mothering: Psychoanalysis and the Sociology of Gender* (Berkeley: University of California Press, 1978), 110.

6. Carol Christ, "Spiritual Quest and Women's Experience," *Womanspirit Rising,* 238.

7. Ellen Brenner, a student of mine at Boston University School of Theology, suggested this to me during class discussion, November 19, 1986.

8. Elizabeth Dodson Gray, *Green Paradise Lost* (Wellesley, Mass., Roundtable Press, 1979), ix.

9. Marie Louise von Franz, a first-generation Jungian analyst and author, has written about the entanglement of men's anima projections and women's sense of themselves:

> The whole problem becomes in one way more, in another less, complicated if we try to concentrate on how the psychology of the feminine and the psychology of the anima are intertwined. . . . Thus some women give in entirely to the anima projection. . . . If he only likes her as an anima figure, she is forced to play the role of the anima. This interreaction can be positive or negative, but the woman is very much affected by the man's anima figure, which brings us to a very primitive and simple and collective level where we cannot separate the features of the anima and real women. Frequently, they are mixed to some extent and react upon each other. (*The Feminine in Fairytales* [Zurich: Spring Publications, 1972], 1–2)

In this helpful clarification in which she speaks of the influence of an individual anima projection on a woman's sense of self, von Franz still misses the powerful influence of the entire patriarchal society on women's sense of self.

10. Jung, *Collected Works,* 7 : 186.
11. Ibid., 187.
12. Ibid., 9(1):98.
13. Ibid., 82.
14. Ibid., 90.
15. Ibid., 99–100.
16. Ibid., 106.
17. See Miller, *Toward a New Psychology of Women,* especially part 1.
18. Jung, *Collected Works,* 9(2): 13.
19. Whitmont, *The Symbolic Quest,* 192.
20. Ernest Becker, *The Denial of Death* (New York: Free Press, 1973), 39–40.
21. Jung, *Collected Works,* 9(1): 107.
22. Ibid.
23. Ulanov, *The Feminine in Jungian Psychology,* 193–94.
24. Ibid., 196.
25. Berger, *The Sacred Canopy,* 37.
26. Whitmont, *The Symbolic Quest,* 179.
27. Jung, *Collected Works,* 9(2):268.
28. Ibid., 14: 178–79.
29. Erich Neumann, *The Origins and History of Consciousness,* Bollingen Series 52 (Princeton: Princeton University Press, 1954), 125n.
30. Jung, *Collected Works,* 9(2): 14.
31. Chodorow, *Mothering,* 169.
32. Jung, *Collected Works,* 7 : 208–9.
33. Ibid.
34. Ibid., 205–6.
35. Emma Jung, *Animus and Anima: Two Essays* (Zurich: Spring Publications, 1957), 20.
36. Ibid. On the following page, however, Emma Jung's words turn decidedly misogynistic. They are a good example of internalized oppression at work, so I quote them here: "It is well known that a really creative faculty of mind is a rare thing in woman. There are many women who have developed their powers of thinking, discrimination, and criticism to a high degree, but there are very few who are mentally creative in the way a man is. It is maliciously said that woman is so lacking in the gift of invention, that if the kitchen spoon had not been invented by a man, we would today still be stirring the soup with a stick!"

INDEX

A

Adler, Alfred, 42, 45
Alienation, 113–14
Amplification, 49
Androcentrism, 10, 80, 125;
  defined, 4, 16; in Jungian
  theory, 97, 99–100, 106–9,
  115–17, 122; in scholarship, 130; in symbol systems, 23, 25; in traditional
  religion, 100
Anima: and female psychology,
  104–14, 118; and the feminine, 32; in Jung, 55, 64,
  97, 99
—and animus: Goldenberg on,
  8; in Jung, 30, 48, 52, 55,
  63–67; Whitmont on, 99
Animus, 5, 64–65, 117–26;
  nature of, 64–65; negative,
  119–21; positive, 121–23;
  -possessed women, 46, 66–
  67, 119–21; projections and
  women's experience, 118
Archetypal images. See Images,
  archetypal

Archetype, x, 34, 81; and archetypal images, 51–52, 91;
  immutability of, 93–94;
  "karma aspect" of, 92; religious nature of, 91–97
Authenticity, 16–17

B

Barbour, Ian, 74
Beauvoir, Simone de, 15
Becker, Ernest, 111–12, 119
Behavior, 13–14, 52, 116
Berger, Peter, 14, 24, 115
Bettelheim, Bruno, 1–2
Body. See Embodiment
Brown, Clifford A., 77
Buber, Martin, 34, 77–79, 95,
  137

C

Castillejo, Irene de, 99
Chodorow, Nancy, 102, 118–19

T

Theology: Christian, 77, 89,
112; feminist, x–xi, 10, 13,
95; Jung's psychology as, xi;
and psychology, 77
Transference, 30, 70–71
Trinity, 37

U

Ulanov, Ann, 2–4, 5, 9, 13,
114–15
Unconscious: archetypal, in
women's lives, 8; reality of, 5
—in Jung: and archetypal images, 28; collective, 7, 22–
23, 51–54, 59, 90, 94; and
creativity, 6; dialogue with,
58, 82; as feminine, 116–
17; and God, 85, 89–91;
and religious experience,
84–85; wisdom of, 36

V

Voices, inner: and individuation, in Jung, 49–50; and
internalized oppression,
18–21, 103, 121. See also
Figures, inner
Vulnerability, 113–14

W

White, Victor, 77
Whitemont, Edward, 57, 99,
110–11, 116
Wholeness, 45, 63, 72, 87, 91
Wolff, Toni, 114
Women: empowerment of, 120;
experience of, 4, 17, 118,
125–26; fear of, 110–14,
124, 126; inner images of,
21; Logos in, 8, 120; as
other, 16, 106, 110; psy-
chology of, x, 5–6, 44–45,
97, 104–14; souls of, 64–
65, 105–6, 117, 118
—selfhood of: 16, 18–21,
100–114; and andro-
centrism, 16–21; and anima
projections, 104; authentic,
search for, 125; "boundary
confusion" in, 102; and individuation, in Jung, 100–
103; and relationality, 103
Worldview: Jungian, 29; and
philosophy of science, 96–
97; prepatriarchal, 23; and
psychological theory, 30, 96;
sexism as a, 14–18; sociology of knowledge as a, 126

Y

Young-Eisendrath, Polly, 7,
17–19, 103